RISE to the CHALLENGE

ASCD MEMBER BOOK

RISE to the CHALLENGE

Designing Rigorous Learning That Maximizes Student Success

JEFF C. MARSHALL

Alexandria, Virginia USA

ASCD

1703 N. Beauregard St. • Alexandria, VA 22311-1714 USA
Phone: 800-933-2723 or 703-578-9600 • Fax: 703-575-5400
Website: www.ascd.org • E-mail: member@ascd.org
Author guidelines: www.ascd.org/write

Ronn Nozoe, *Interim CEO & Executive Director;* Stefani Roth, *Publisher;* Genny Ostertag, *Director, Content Acquisitions;* Allison Scott, *Acquisitions Editor;* Julie Houtz, *Director, Book Editing & Production;* Miriam Calderone, *Editor;* Judi Connelly, *Senior Art Director;* Donald Ely, *Associate Art Director;* Keith Demmons, *Production Designer;* Mike Kalyan, *Director, Production Services;* Trinay Blake, *E-Publishing Specialist*

PAPERBACK ISBN: 978-1-4166-2798-2   ASCD product #120007
PDF E-BOOK ISBN: 978-1-4166-2800-2; see Books in Print for other formats.
Quantity discounts are available: e-mail programteam@ascd.org or call 800-933-2723, ext. 5773, or 703-575-5773. For desk copies, go to www.ascd.org/deskcopy.

ASCD Member Book No. FY19-8B (Jul. 2019 PSI+). ASCD Member Books mail to Premium (P), Select (S), and Institutional Plus (I+) members on this schedule: Jan, PSI+; Feb, P; Apr, PSI+; May, P; Jul, PSI+; Aug, P; Sep, PSI+; Nov, PSI+; Dec, P. For current details on membership, see www.ascd.org/membership.

Library of Congress Cataloging-in-Publication Data is available for this title.
Library of Congress Control Number:2019942388

27 26 25 24 23 22 21 20 19   1 2 3 4 5 6 7 8 9 10 11 12

Designing Rigorous Learning That Maximizes Student Success

Acknowledgments

It is with great thanks that I pause to appreciate the support and inspiration that so many have provided in my life. My wife, Wendy, and my children, Anna and Ben, remind me through their daily living of the importance of learning and the doors that are opened with a strong education. Over my career, I have had the opportunity to work with, interact with, and be inspired by many extraordinary people. I especially give thanks to Ena Shelley, George Peterson, Greg Lineweaver, Rachelle Savitz, Bob Horton, Danny Alston, Julie Smart, and Kimberly Montrose-Thomas. Each of you has provided a unique set of supports, including edits, honest feedback, inspiration, examples, and perspective. Finally, thanks to my parents, who persisted and believed that all their effort helping to guide my writing over the years, poor as it was at times, would eventually pay off.

Introduction: Using Challenge to Maximize Academic Excellence

We as educators are asked to excel with all our students each and every day, despite the many obstacles placed in our way. So what must occur for us all to succeed?

Challenge. Perhaps nothing is more critical to the success of students, teachers, and schools. A bold claim, but the pages that follow provide substantiating evidence alongside insights on how to maximize challenge, and thus success, for all the students in your classroom.

I recently realized that I, along with a great many other educators, have been asking the wrong question of teachers: "Do you provide a challenging and rigorous learning environment for students?" The unequivocal answer is always "Yes!"—but then, no rational teachers would admit to *not* providing a challenging learning environment, even if it were true. Questions with truisms for answers—"Do all teachers desire to be effective in the classroom?" "Can all students learn?" "Should learning promote critical thinking and 21st century skills?"—tend to affirm the status quo. So I began restating the question as follows: "What evidence do you have that challenge and rigor are consistently present in your classroom?" Or to make it even more tangible, "Where were challenge and rigor most visible in today's lesson?" I find that teachers consistently and confidently proclaim that challenge and rigor are central to their teaching and learning, yet frequently go silent when asked to offer tangible supporting evidence.

Moving from blanket proclamations of challenging instruction to an evidence-packed understanding of what challenge looks like, feels like, and sounds like in the classroom is the shift at the heart of this book. Once we know what we are looking for, we can chart a course to modify our teaching so that challenge, rigor, and excellence are consistently present in our classrooms. Asking for evidence to support claims of challenging instruction generates a conversation that is more honest and more closely aligned to day-to-day practice than simply asking a yes-or-no question.

Given limited time and energy, it is essential that we prioritize our professional growth to effectively guide student learning. I realize that many are coming to this conversation tired and skeptical, suffering from initiative fatigue. It feels as though we try every new (and old) thing, only to quickly move on to the latest idea, not knowing if what we were doing before would yield results given sufficient time to work. Without careful examination and appropriate implementation, many initiatives are doomed from the start.

So how do we move from our current status quo to a pursuit of excellence that allows all students to succeed? First, we must realize that there is no magic bullet; we won't wake up tomorrow and find all our challenges replaced by a happily-ever-after experience. Highly effective instructional practice takes time, intentionality, and effort. We must move away from trying to do it all, which results in rarely doing anything well. Instead, we must focus on aspects we can actually change.

The Pareto principle, more commonly referred to as the 80/20 rule, provides some critical insights here. The rule states that 80 percent (give or take) of effects can be attributed to 20 percent of causes. In the context of education, I argue that roughly 80 percent of student success comes from about 20 percent of the efforts made by teachers. Sadly, the converse seems true as well: that nearly 80 percent of our efforts in evaluation and professional development result in roughly a 20 percent shift toward student achievement. My team's research (Marshall, Smart, & Alston, 2016) confirms this premise and has shown that many of the factors that we think are critical in the classroom actually have very little effect on student success.

Write down your answer to the following question: in 15 words or fewer, what factors do you think are most responsible for maximally effective teaching? When I ask this question in workshops, the following terms tend to pop up: *strong relationships, a growth mindset, passionate teaching, strong management, effective assessment, strong content knowledge, student-centered teaching,* and *effective implementation of instructional strategies.* All these ideas are important on some level (some much more so than others), but the most important one—and the focus of this book—is consistently absent: *a culture of challenge that supports and inspires all students.*

The Teacher Intentionality Practice Scale (TIPS)

In my previous book, *The Highly Effective Teacher: 7 Classroom-Tested Practices That Foster Student Success* (Marshall, 2016), I argue that teacher effectiveness can be boiled down to the following elements of the Teacher Intentionality Practice Scale (TIPS) framework:

TIP 1: A coherent, connected learning progression

TIP 2: Strategies, resources, and technologies that enhance learning

TIP 3: A safe, respectful, well-organized learning environment

TIP 4: Challenging, rigorous learning experiences (the focus of this book)

TIP 5: Interactive, thoughtful learning

TIP 6: A creative, problem-solving culture

TIP 7: Monitoring, assessment, and feedback that guide and inform instruction and learning.

Although it may seem reductive to argue that effective teaching can be condensed to seven characteristics, research suggests that fully 55 percent of the variance in teacher effectiveness can be explained by TIPs 4–7 alone (Marshall et al., 2016).

The first three characteristics of highly effective practice—a coherent, connected learning progression; strategies, resources, and technologies that enhance learning; and a safe, respectful, well-organized learning environment—reflect the nuts and bolts of how we teach. It makes sense that new teachers wrestle with these aspects of practice more frequently than veteran teachers, for whom they often become routine. In the following sections, I provide a summary of each of the seven TIPs.

TIP 1: A Coherent, Connected Learning Progression

Coherence begins with ensuring that your standards, objectives, lessons, and assessments are all in alignment. It's wise not to assume that just because a lesson is published in a textbook or on the internet it is clear, logically sequenced, and properly aligned to relevant objectives. When I conduct a Google search for energy lesson plans, a common topic in science, how many of the 137,000,000 resulting hits meet my needs? I have seen compare-and-contrast lessons consisting of a PowerPoint slide highlighting differences and similarities between various forms of energy—a lower-order activity that does not meet the higher-order target intended in a compare-and-contrast lesson. Instead, students should be asked to explore, test, demonstrate, and discover that energy largely fits within two major categories: kinetic and potential. Once they realize this, they can begin to relate other forms of energy, such as mechanical, chemical, or sound, to these broader categories.

In addition to being coherent, lessons should connect learning to students' lives and to the big ideas. Otherwise students are just learning isolated facts. Knowledge retention is much more difficult when students can't tie that knowledge to real-life experiences. Using well-crafted essential questions is a great way to start integrating lessons into the bigger picture.

TIP 2: Strategies, Resources, and Technologies That Enhance Learning

When we are strategic in our instruction, we focus on strategies, resources, and technologies that deeply and meaningfully engage the learner. To increase student-centered learning, we should ask such questions as the following: "To what extent are students provided with concrete experiences before abstract ideas?" "To what degree are students active in the learning process?" "To what extent do students go beyond just mimicking or verifying what the teacher has shown?" Strategies may include scaffolding learning experiences that start with exploration of concepts, ideas, and questions before any formal explanation is given or modeled so that the learning is increasingly inquiry-based.

Modern technological advances have led many boards of education, administrators, and teachers to believe that technology will close the achievement gap, increase learning for all, and basically solve all education challenges. Unfortunately, computers are too often used as little more than glorified overhead projectors or word processors. When used strategically, technologies are transformative and purposeful. Common technologies such as Google Classroom can be either ordinary or transformative, depending on implementation. When students use technology collaboratively, through peer editing or by sharing documents, the final product is often superior and has greater potential to significantly increase learning.

TIP 3: A Safe, Respectful, Well-Organized Learning Environment

There is a big difference between efficiency and effectiveness. As teachers, we want learning to be *effective*. As far as procedures and general management, we strive for a fluid, predictable, and *efficient* classroom that creates a respectful, collaborative environment. A well-managed classroom does not improve learning by itself. Rather, it sets the stage for success. Using instructional time wisely, paying attention to pacing and transitions, and establishing and following successful routines are the first steps in achieving a well-managed classroom. If consistently followed, positive habits established early on will save enormous time and energy as the school year progresses.

Effective teachers cultivate a respectful and collaborative learning environment. This includes being proactive with behavior management; maintaining a patient, encouraging, and listening environment; and being supportive, respectful, and approachable to students. Learning and collaboration are stifled when students fear how others will respond if they make a mistake or interpret something differently from others. Many will choose not to engage at all or will play it safe, providing lower-quality responses. It is up to the teacher to lead, model, and provide an unquestionably safe place where all can take risks and learn.

If the first three TIPS focus on pedagogical knowledge—the practices and art of teaching—the last four focus on pedagogical content knowledge (PCK): successfully engaging students with specific content. We have all heard of teachers who, though clearly brilliant, were ineffective in making content accessible to all learners. Great teachers can take the challenging and make it attainable for all. To paraphrase the late, great physicist Richard Feynman, if you can't explain something in simple terms, you don't understand it.

TIP 4: Challenging, Rigorous Learning Experiences

The practice of identifying, promoting, and refining the challenge, rigor, and excellence of classroom instruction on a daily basis is the focus of this book. This practice is where the greatest variance in performance of highly effective teachers can be explained. Although most teachers will say they provide their students with challenging and rigorous learning experiences, few are able to convincingly identify the challenge and rigor present in their lessons.

This book seeks to help teachers develop challenging, rigorous, and excellent learning experiences for students.

TIP 5: Interactive, Thoughtful Learning

Highly effective classrooms seek to balance the *intrapersonal* and the *interpersonal*. If the instructional focus is overly intrapersonal, students may have trouble understanding perspectives outside their own and fail to appreciate the synergistic effects of collaboration; if it's overly interpersonal, students may have trouble developing self-sufficiency and learning to problem-solve on their own.

When we give students a test or challenge their understanding, we want them to be thoughtful and to exercise metacognition as they develop their knowledge. To this end, it is vital that we provide students with a richly engaging culture. Questions should stimulate thinking and participation with others, and interactions should be conversational and motivating. It is our responsibility as teachers to ensure that the purpose and relevance of learning experiences are clear to students.

TIP 6: A Creative, Problem-Solving Culture

Both creativity and problem solving are vital for success in today's world, where we must work with the millions of vast data sets available to us online. To equip students for this reality, we need to foster a creative and inquisitive learning environment where students tackle open-ended problems and consider multiple perspectives. With new information constantly coming to light in our interconnected age, students must learn how to go about understanding the intent and purpose of what they encounter and whether to modify prior conceptions.

TIP 7: Monitoring, Assessment, and Feedback That Guide and Inform Instruction and Learning

The research on formative assessment is clear: checking in multiple times with *all* students in every class has a positive effect on achievement. Where there is proper formative assessment, the results of summative assessment shouldn't come as any surprise and should reflect student growth. Diagnostic assessment that probes prior knowledge, often categorized alongside formative assessment, allows teachers to establish a benchmark starting point for individual students, classes, and groups of students. Understanding prior knowledge helps teachers to address any misconceptions students may have about subject-matter content.

How to Read This Book

This book is divided into four chapters. Chapter 1 helps to contextualize the problems today's teachers face as they try to provide students with challenging learning experiences. Chapter 2 provides a series of conversations to illuminate how the culture we create in our classroom can influence the pursuit of challenge. Chapter 3 explores various instructional approaches to ensuring that students are challenged as they learn. Finally, Chapter 4 shows how to enact challenging lessons and work through common obstacles.

Throughout the book I've included "Stop to Reflect" sections offering concrete actions, reflection questions, and recommendations for further growth to help you process information and apply it to your own practice. As you read, jot down notes for later reference and underline areas you want to revisit. In the margins, write questions that you wish to explore further. Because we are all at different places in our careers and have differing needs, the ideas presented here will not be of the same value or effectiveness to every reader. The purpose is to get you thinking, reflecting, questioning, and talking about learning so you can better sculpt instruction to provide students with transformative classroom experiences.

Whether you read this book cover to cover or dip in and out, on your own or in a study group, I encourage you to constantly assess the potential of what you read to improve your students' learning. In the business world, return on investment (ROI) is relatively easy to measure. In education, this task is considerably harder. Has student engagement risen? Has academic performance improved? Has the value of learning increased? Have students begun to challenge themselves at a deeper level? All these questions must be carefully considered before we can know the ROI of a given practice or strategy.

I hope you choose to challenge yourself as you assess, reflect on, and then act on improving your own practice. The reward of such effort will be extraordinary!

1
Wicked Solutions for Wicked Problems

Reflect on your best days as a teacher. What made the difference in your success or your students' success? Was it something within your control or outside of it? Now think about a day that did not go as well as you had hoped. What was responsible for the disappointment?

One of the key differences between good and exemplary teachers is that the latter realize that they play an essential role in the success of their students. Despite district mandates, high poverty rates, apathetic students, unsupportive parents, constant school interruptions, or any other such external factors, exemplary teachers begin by acknowledging that *all* students can and must succeed. Any other option is unacceptable.

Simply put, teaching isn't for the weak. In fact, I suggest that highly effective teaching is one of our society's most wicked problems. Truly wicked problems (sometimes referred to as "sticky problems" or "Gordian knots") don't have easy solutions, and no manual exists to definitively resolve them. There is no pill you can take to surmount learning differences, achievement gaps, differing life experiences, and so forth. Just as with other wicked problems like poverty, homelessness, inadequate health care, climate change, and violence, educators seeking to foster highly effective learning for all students are in search of wicked solutions.

So much of what educators do is evaluated and measured despite having little effect on achievement. Requiring that lesson objectives or curriculum standards be posted on the front board, for example —I have yet to see any data showing that this practice increases student learning. No student really cares what the standard is;

explicitly stating it does not help to engage students and takes up precious board space. The standard's purpose is to help the teacher and instructional leaders guide and frame the lesson and curriculum. A good alternative would be to post each lesson standard on a clipboard and hang it by the door for any visitors to see (or better yet, on Google Classroom) and use the now-vacant board space for a well-conceived essential question that frames how students will be engaged. When answered, this question will sufficiently address the standard and objective(s).

Our attempts to solve the wicked problem of highly effective teaching and learning have been thwarted in recent years, partly because we have fallen prey to confirmation bias—the tendency to selectively search for and consider information that confirms our beliefs. This bias abounds in all areas of society, and the internet has only made it more prevalent. Search engines and social media use algorithms to tailor content to individual users' interests. This is extremely helpful to advertisers, of course, but it also creates a more polarized society where we are exposed only to data that align with our beliefs, resulting in a very unbalanced perspective. Unless we consciously challenge our beliefs and assumptions and seek differing opinions and ideas, this tendency will continue. To begin moving beyond confirmation bias in education, we need to seek out opposing viewpoints that challenge our thinking and actions. Challenge is the key lever to help us *and* our students engage, learn, and thrive.

The following sections contextualize just what today's teachers are up against in their effort to provide challenge—and offer some insights and guidance for tackling the wicked problem of excelling with *all* students.

Setting Objectives: Making Today Better Than Yesterday

Although it may seem simplistic, working to make every day better than the day before would transform our education system. If every teacher were consistently and significantly better at the job with each passing day, our classes would quickly become extraordinary places. To consistently and systematically improve requires developing strong habits and intentional behaviors. This does not necessarily mean working longer or harder, but it does entail consistently reflecting upon and improving instructional habits.

To intentionally make today better than yesterday, begin by targeting a specific habit or strategy you seek to change. Write it down so you remember to act upon it. Identify the steps necessary to make this habit or strategy integral to your work or to students' experiences. Remember that if the goal involves your students, you need to work consistently with them to make it a part of their learning. As the habit becomes routine, it will become automated in the teaching and learning process and you can begin tackling the next most important obstacle to raising the levels of challenge, rigor, and excellence in your classroom. The difficulty often arises when we tackle too many changes or goals at once: students, teachers, and leaders can rightfully become confused about what is truly important. Valuing everything as critically important ensures you will master nothing while becoming increasingly frustrated at the lack of progress.

The goals that you target should be personal to your setting, students, and needs. One example would be to set a goal of incorporating formative assessment every 10–15 minutes (or after every three or four slides during a PowerPoint presentation) to assess whether and where students are struggling. Formative assessment has repeatedly been shown to have one of the largest effect sizes of any instructional intervention for improving academic success (Hattie, 2009).

Improving your questioning techniques is another worthy goal. It is easy to fall into a pattern of asking mostly factual recall questions, which tend to squelch excitement and curiosity. While factual questions are necessary at times, an overreliance on them misses the vast array of questions that could engage your students and enliven your classroom. Great questions stimulate deeper thinking by piquing student curiosity, imagination, and wonder. Having a powerful set of verbs handy to guide your questioning to higher levels of Bloom's taxonomy or Webb's Depth of Knowledge (DoK) is a good starting point (Anderson et al., 2001; Hess, Carlock, Jones, & Walkup, 2009). We all are adept at asking basic knowledge or recall questions ("Who was the villain in the story?" "What is three times four?" "Where did the scene take place?"), but we need intentional practice in raising the cognitive rigor of our classrooms by using a more open-ended approach ("How could you improve . . . ?" "What if . . . ?" "How does . . . make you feel?" "How might you . . . ?" "What happens when . . . ?").

A first step in asking more powerful and engaging questions might be to write on an index card each day the three or four most engaging questions you want to explore with your students. These could be essential questions ("What makes a hero?"), argumentative questions ("Is there better a way to do this?" "Isn't it possible that . . . ?"), personal/affective questions ("How did this make you feel?" "When have you felt similar?"), or analytical questions ("How can we understand the underlying causes?" "What occurred?"). The point is to design questions for increased challenge, not just to meet standards or curriculum objectives.

To make your improvements last, you must be consistent in your efforts and hold yourself accountable. Perhaps you can find a partner who also wants to change a habit and work together to hold each other accountable. Once new habits have become ingrained, work on making small refinements to them while beginning to identify and then tackling a new obstacle. If you seek to make today better than yesterday, then you should always be able to identify and reflect upon the habit that you are currently working to improve.

STOP TO REFLECT

- What are three to five habits that you want to change or improve? (If you are unsure what those habits may be, read further and make a note to revisit this section.)
- Which one of the identified habits is paramount to your success with your students?
- What are some steps you can take to acquire or improve that habit?
- When and how can you address each of these steps?
- Are you clear with students about your goal and consistent in your work toward meeting it?
- Who holds you accountable for meeting your goal?

The most difficult part of changing or improving a habit is getting started. If your goal is to ask better questions, for example, make it easy on yourself at first: come up with one engaging question for tomorrow. Then, come up with one highly engaging question for each prep that you have the next day. Incremental change is more likely to result in success. If you are seeking to build better relationships with your students, begin by intentionally devoting 15–30 seconds to a different student each day. As time passes, you will get better at carving out intentional time to interact with two students per class, then three, and so on without interfering with instruction and learning.

So, what will you start today? Write it down along with the first action you need to take. If you want your students to get better, then you must be willing to challenge yourself to get better as well. Without your willingness to change, things will remain exactly the way they were yesterday.

Challenge and Stress

A survey of incoming freshmen at UCLA showed a dramatic increase in students responding that they felt overwhelmed by all they had to do during the previous year (Eagan, 2016), with 18 percent responding yes in 1985, 29 percent in 2010, and 41 percent in 2016. Our adrenaline and cortisol levels spike when we're significantly stressed and only return to normal levels when the stress subsides (Talbott, 2007). When our stress-response system is chronically activated, we are at greater risk for anxiety, depression, sleep problems, suppressed immune system, memory and concentration impairment, and weight gain.

Anxiety is the most common mental health disorder, affecting approximately one-third of all adolescents in the United States

(Merikangas et al., 2010). When our anxiety is out of control, we tend to overestimate the danger of stressors and underestimate our ability to cope. Although it is felt across all socioeconomic categories, anxiety tends to affect various groups differently. Anxiety in students from more affluent households, for example, frequently manifests itself in the form of perfectionism, a fear of failure, and a sense that their efforts are never sufficient (Luthar & Latendresse, 2005).

Some may say that the rise in stress and anxiety among students means we need to lower expectations rather than increase them. I believe the opposite: that we have overprotected our students from unknowns and uncomfortable situations, resulting in bubble-wrapped kids. We tend to set up perfect, idealized learning situations that are unrealistic, so when students are confronted with the messy real world, they are easily overwhelmed. A "helicopter parent" society has resulted in students not knowing how to work through dilemmas, unknowns, or awkward situations. Well-intentioned overseers swoop down to save students when anything remotely troubling surfaces. Schools only make matters worse by leaning increasingly toward avoidance-based strategies rather than exposure-based ones. When Ethan and Silva don't work well with others, we allow them to work alone instead of helping them build the capacity to function better in collaborative settings.

To flip this paradigm, we need to sometimes place students in uncomfortable situations. In this way, students can learn to confront fears, anxieties, and challenges of increasing complexity without shutting down or feeling the need to run. If we truly want to encourage resiliency and perseverance, then we must create scaffolded learning opportunities in this area. It is far easier to talk about the need for students to be resilient than it is to model it and hold students accountable for it.

Distractions

There is little doubt that we are becoming more distracted as a society. On the road, drivers demonstrate this by weaving back and forth wildly while attending to the continuous pings of e-mail and social media apps. (I felt the painful reality of that personally one day several years ago, when a distracted motorist struck me while I was riding my bike.) Although inattentiveness seems pervasive in the classroom, the research is mixed. A recent *Time* story (McSpadden, 2015) stated that our attention spans waned from 12 seconds on average in 2000 to 8 seconds on average in 2015. If true, this places us just behind goldfish, which are reported to have an attention span of 9 seconds. It appears that classroom lectures of 30 minutes or an hour are a complete waste of time.

Or are they? Further investigation (Bradbury, 2016) reveals that these data come from a 2015 Microsoft report stating that the average person spends about 8 seconds on a website. It would be an inaccurate leap to extrapolate too broadly from such a finding. There are myriad reasons why people click off pages—because the sites are unhelpful, for example, or because the information sought is quickly found. Perhaps the real story is that people have improved by about 30 percent in their ability to filter and find targeted information. It could also be true that we are using the internet more often to quickly access simple facts (e.g., sports scores, word meanings, calendars) than was the case in 2000.

More germane to the conversation is research from Middendorf and Kalish (1996) finding that attention and resulting performance drop dramatically when lectures exceed 15 minutes, with a significant increase in students checking out for a minute or more after that time (Bunce, Flens, & Neiles, 2010). Even so, far more consequential to student attention are the teacher's skills and abilities (Bligh, 1998; Bradbury, 2016). Just think back to examples in your own life; in some classes, you would probably willingly engage for hours, whereas other times you tuned out immediately.

We know our students are increasingly anxious and increasingly distracted. So how can we take positive steps forward while consistently challenging them?

The Need to Know

Challenging students means pushing them beyond their comfort zone in developmentally appropriate ways. To do this successfully, we must remain cognizant of student cognitive load. Without going into a full course on cognitive psychology, *cognitive load* is essentially the maximum amount of short-term or working memory that is available to us at any given time. Give or take a little, we can work with about seven elements (e.g., letters, words, numbers) at once. Our working-memory capacity does not change much as we get older or acquire more knowledge: as our expertise in an area increases, so does our ability to chunk (e.g., seeing three groups of 5 as three elements rather than 15), categorize (e.g., placing vowels in one group and consonants in another), and draw from long-term memory (e.g., knowing that you have a dog or have been to the beach). We move items from short-term memory to long-term memory through rehearsal and use, and it is easiest when we can link them to prior experiences or knowledge (schema).

A *need to know* is essential to the process of knowledge retention. Students don't usually attend class eager to learn about photosynthesis or how to say *eat* in Spanish. Instead, they come innately curious about the world around them: they wonder why the leaves on trees are mostly green but turn colors during the fall, or how they might communicate with a relative in Spain. Too often, we start and end learning by focusing on computational fluency: memorizing vocabulary in world languages or the multiplication tables in math, learning facts and dates in social studies, defining concepts in science. Instead, we should begin by giving students real-world dilemmas to solve, creating a need to know that inspires them to learn the fundamentals. When we engage students first and truly get them exploring major ideas before we deliver facts, content knowledge improves for all students, narrowing the achievement gap in the process (Marshall, 2013; Marshall & Alston, 2014; Marshall, Smart, & Alston, 2017). Memorization and computational fluency are important, but the amount and sequencing of both should be intentionally addressed.

Lowering the Cognitive Load

When putting exploration before skill proficiency, it is important to lower the cognitive load where possible so short-term memory can focus on areas requiring the most rigor. For instance, when beginning to write for deeper meaning, many students struggle with the vocabulary necessary to enrich their writing. A vocabulary continuum, either student- or teacher-created, can provide words with different strengths of connotation so students can incorporate more powerful verbs or richer adjectives in their sentences. Give examples of sentence variety to help students build the complexity of their writing. Positively reinforce students when they go beyond provided examples and incorporate rich vocabulary or vibrant sentence variations.

In math class, students could come up with examples of real-world problems that illustrate the concepts being studied. For instance, when studying percentages, students could calculate the tip for a meal, the discount on a sweater, or the tax on a purchase. Reward those who can tie examples to previous concepts. If students have 10 problems for homework, the first 8 could focus on building computational fluency, and the final 2 could be an opportunity for them to extend their knowledge. Just remember that students should practice computational fluency *after* they have explored and grasped the concept.

In history class, as you begin to investigate events, you can provide a list of historical figures to study and reward students who find additional figures related to the event or time period. Emphasize the importance of synthesizing the historical understanding from multiple perspectives (e.g., World War II from the perspectives of people in Japan, England, Germany, and Russia, or from the perspective of an American homemaker, farmer, military family, or politician).

There is a sweet spot in learning. If the process is too easy, then students get bored. If it is too hard, they can become overwhelmed. We tend to see students who appear very apathetic at either end of the challenge continuum.

The 40 Percent Rule

Centuries ago, Horace wrote the phrase *aequam memento rebus in arduis servare mentem:* "remember when life's path is steep to keep your mind even." In our increasingly distracted society, it is imperative that we learn how to focus better. According to the "40 percent rule," whenever we think we are mentally, physically, or emotionally spent, we have actually reached only about 40 percent of our capacity. It is preposterous to expect our students (or ourselves) to perform at 100 percent mental or intellectual effort 100 percent of the time, but we need to learn that running from difficult situations is not a solution for growth, either. Whether in sports, arts, or academics, our greatest achievements often require a bit of hardship.

Think about where you want students to focus most in your class and make your expectations clear to them. Begin by establishing a benchmark to assess existing student stress levels. This can be done very quickly through a brief survey that asks students to respond using a Likert scale (strongly agree, agree, neutral, disagree, strongly disagree) to statements such as "I feel comfortable sharing in class," "I am OK not always having the right answer," and "I feel the work in the class is challenging yet achievable." Depending on your purpose, you may wish to make the survey anonymous. Once you identify key stressors for students, you can begin to develop strategies for minimizing them (e.g., by moving a test or deadline back by a day) and help students develop coping strategies.

Moving Past the Status Quo

Rigor and challenge are often expressed in terms of speed and agility relative to a given knowledge base or skill set. However, true challenge requires us to completely rethink an idea, swimming against very powerful and sometimes antagonistic forces. Nicolaus Copernicus stood against the Church and society when he proposed that Earth revolved around the sun rather than the other way around—a reconceptualization that in turn made humanity rethink how planetary bodies move. It is worth noting that his work was published 66 years before Galileo used the first telescope in 1609.

It is easy to say that you'll never be as revolutionary as Copernicus, but all individuals are capable of learning to take static facts and figures and use them in new ways. In so doing, we become the next authors, musicians, leaders, doctors, and teachers. We need individuals who will challenge the status quo if we want to make the world, community, or school a bit better than it was yesterday. Deviating from the norm does not mean that students are no longer responsible for learning essential skills such as vocabulary or basic arithmetic. Instead, it is about reexamining the frequency and duration of such learning.

Know your goals and build a plan for pushing against the status quo. As an example, you might choose to provide students with "create time" every Friday, during which they can freely explore a matter that excites them but that you have not fully explained to them. In a science/engineering class, students might create a new product for an "Invention Convention" later in the year. In other classes, they might choreograph their own dances, write their own plays, or create their own documentaries on historical figures or events. For many students, this flexibility will be exciting and freeing, while for others it will be a bit terrifying at first. Most will be at least a bit uncomfortable at the beginning, not quite knowing where or how to begin. Give them some time (depending on the grade level or complexity of task) to think it through or jot down ideas. Then, provide those who need it with a framework to help guide their process. Some students may need more support here than others. Students must identify the topic, product, or idea before they can begin outlining, prototyping, or developing a procedure.

You may prefer to infuse smaller pockets of create time into the day-to-day learning process. In math class, for instance, where we are often focused on absolutes and single solutions, we might provide frequent opportunities for students to learn how to estimate solutions that don't have a single answer (e.g., projecting a family or company budget). After all, the real world is a mix of absolutes and approximations. When engineers design structures, they always "over-design" to allow for unforeseen events; similarly, when builders estimate costs, they always seek to provide a cushion for cost overruns.

Real-world learning contexts can encourage students to push beyond the status quo of abstract and sterile computations. Here's an example of an exercise that challenges students to think deeply and in a real-world context about an estimation activity using basic arithmetic skills:

> You are a homebuilding team, and a client would like you to build a variation of a type of home you have built several times over the past two years. You know that your total cost before any profit has typically run about $185,000 for the 2,400-square-foot home. The client would like to add 2 feet across the entire back of the home and wants to know how much it will cost.
>
> Remember that you need to make a profit on the home to keep your business running, but if your price is unreasonably high, you will lose your client to another builder. [Note: a 10 percent profit may be a reasonable target, but it would be good for students to consider what their profit margin needs to be and then see if their estimate has made them competitive with others.] Each team will come up with a price that it must justify to the client in a two-minute presentation.

A few details that may or may not be helpful:

1. This is a single-story house.
2. The house is approximately 60 feet wide and 40 feet deep.
3. The requested addition will add about 20 square feet to the kitchen, and the rest of the added space will be in general living space (e.g., a living room or bedroom).
4. The new lot cost is $42,000 versus $35,000 for the prior homes built.
5. Because of a building boom across the country, construction costs have increased by about 15 percent since your last homebuilding project.

STOP TO REFLECT

- What are three opportunities in an upcoming lesson for allowing students to go beyond the norm?
- Where do you tend to follow the status quo, and where do you tend to push against it?
- Should you change any of your current stances toward student learning? Why or why not?
- What would it take to make such changes?

Playing in the Box

It's fun to think outside the box, but we also need to be grounded in reality. Any solutions to problems that we devise must still conform to conditions in the box that we are required to play in. We can reshape the box a bit, but we can't just toss it away. We must address the state or national standards, for example, and we must comply with district, state, or federal mandates. Yet our process is also bounded by our own perceptions, which can at times limit our progress.

Time and Timing

We are also bound by the time we are given to interact with our students. The Greeks had two words for time: *chronos,* meaning chronological time, and *kairos,* meaning time that is opportune or right. In the business world, timing in the latter sense accounts for approximately 42 percent of the difference between whether a company succeeds or fails (Grant, 2017). Finding *kairos* in the classroom— the proper timing and sequencing of learning to maximize student achievement—is critical for success.

Do you think you have even greater success with your students when given less time? This may seem absurd on the surface, but adding time to the school day has not clearly been shown to improve student achievement, even for those who are behind academically. The research is mixed and often entangled with other possible factors, such as higher expectations. Instead of simply fighting for more time, we should focus on how we use the time we have. The Program for International Student Assessment (PISA) shows schools in the United States to be about average among developed nations in terms of time spent on science, mathematics, and language arts each week. Students in countries with well-regarded school systems like Finland and Japan actually spend less time on these subjects than do U.S. students. Any increase in time allotted to students would need to be coupled with more meaningful learning opportunities to work (Organisation for Economic Co-operation and Development [OECD], 2015). In fact, a longer school year may be helpful. This makes intuitive sense, since we know that there tends to be a precipitous learning loss for students during the summer months.

But again, just adding time is not the answer if it will only be squandered, particularly after state testing has occurred. We have seen a consistent trend in the quality of instruction increasing from the beginning of the year until early in the third quarter, after which it drops steeply as teachers focus on preparation for state or national tests at the expense of learning (Cian, Marshall, & Qian, 2018). The last few weeks of school are often filled with parties, movie days, or "free" days. If this is consistently the case, I would argue for shortening rather than lengthening the school year.

We err when we think we must craft every lesson to fit a given class period. Some lessons may take 130 minutes to complete, with each day's dismissal bell simply denoting an intermission; others may be short enough to allow the last 15 minutes of class time to be used to set the stage for whatever comes next tomorrow. Unfortunately, it's all too common to find students staring into their phones after completing a quiz that only took half of the allotted class time to complete. Effective teachers find ways to turn idle blocks of time into meaningful learning opportunities.

Review your essential purpose or goal for students and identify any constraints that are holding them back from maximal success. Realize that not every frustration is an obstacle. If you don't have evidence that something is holding students back in some way, remove it from your list. Remember that many teachers thrive with the same constraints in place as you, so success is certainly possible. Henry Ford famously said, "Whether you think you can or think you can't, you're right." You can't just get rid of standards, double instructional time, or dispense with district mandates, so focus instead on using standards to frame instruction, using instructional time more effectively, and complying with mandates in ways that don't distract you from enhancing your students' success.

Who Am I? Where Am I Going?

This chapter explored the wicked problem of challenging and excelling with all our students. This is certainly no easy feat, but it's manageable if you develop and implement a thoughtful, intentional plan. Whether you aim to build students' resiliency and perseverance or move past the status quo of low challenge, the chapters that follow look at the key linchpins of culture, design, assessment, and implementation associated with challenge and excellence in your classroom. These elements, when coordinated together, provide a powerful framework to build upon.

Go through your current student roster and score each student on academic success and challenge. (If you are doing this in the summer or very early in the year, you may want to use last year's roster and think retrospectively on your interactions with students.) Use the following scores:

- S1: highly successful
- S2: moderately successful
- S3: not successful
- C1: consistently and highly challenged
- C2: sometimes challenged
- C3: rarely or not challenged

For this exercise, *highly successful* means strong academic achievement and *highly challenged* means students are pushed to question, discover, and explore beyond their comfort zones or current abilities. What metrics will you use to arrive at your scores? Students' current grades? Their scores on standardized tests? Be sure that you have a cutoff for each category and your metrics reflect something that you or your district highly values. I recommend using a spreadsheet for easy analysis. What patterns do you see? Where did most of your students fall? Who is not being challenged? Who is not succeeding? Be careful not to draw conclusions that will curb further growth, such as dismissing students' potential for improvement because they have a difficult family life or different cultural background. In the next chapter, an entire section is devoted to how labels and expectations affect student performance. Think through why students may be receiving the scores you determine, then begin to unravel what your next steps will be.

STOP TO REFLECT

- Where do you tend to follow the status quo?
- What is important enough for you to speak out about?
- What would an observer in your class see if asked to identify where challenge, rigor, and excellence are present?
- Where would you like to improve in this area?
- What is stressful to you or your students?
- Where can you lower stress, and where is stress necessary for your goals?
- How and when should you challenge the status quo in your classroom?
- How can you use time more efficiently?

- What two or three things do you value most as an educator?
- How does your teaching support these values?

Summing Up

This chapter challenged you to intentionally clarify who you are and where you are going as a classroom leader. Remember, as you pursue a path toward greater challenge, it is important that you challenge your own thinking. After all, how can you challenge students authentically if you aren't willing to challenge yourself?

2

Creating a
Culture of
Challenge

When friends or family come over for dinner, we straighten up a bit and set the table beforehand, preparing the right environment for the evening ahead. Likewise, the environment or culture that you establish in your classroom provides the foundation to support subsequent student learning. In this chapter, I illuminate how the culture we create in our classroom can influence the pursuit of challenge.

To develop a strong, positive classroom culture, we must ask four essential questions:

1. Where's the beef?
2. Where's the love?
3. Where's the value?
4. Where's the power?

Where's the Beef?

One of the best conference sessions that I ever attended built on the old Wendy's restaurant slogan "Where's the beef?" The "beef" in this context referred to higher-order thinking skills. The session challenged teachers to explore where the beef was in their lessons. In the absence of a rich curriculum that challenges students to think deeply, the best we can hope for is a nurturing environment with little substance.

Challenge, rigor, and focus reside along a continuum. To check your success in these areas, ask the following questions:

- What key standards did I address during the past week?
- How much of expected student performance reflected lower-level thinking (listing, defining, restating)? Mid-level thinking (applying)? Higher-level thinking (comparing and contrasting, analyzing, creating)?
- Where and how could I have pushed student learning to higher levels?
- Where in my lesson did I challenge students to go beyond basic or lower-level expectations?

Where's the Love?

Consider the relational aspects of your classroom. Do all students feel included and appreciated? What do you do to ensure that they do? How do you include those who are shy or not confident in their work? How do you work to build an inclusive environment for all, regardless of ethnicity, gender, or ability? Even teachers who tend to thrive in the area of relationships can struggle with these kinds of questions.

Cultivating relationships doesn't mean teachers should be overly permissive or allow students to run roughshod over them or others. Rather, caring classes provide firmness and fairness without being mean or condescending. This fairness creates an environment where students feel included and can see their potential. Realize that fairness is not the same thing as equal treatment. This distinction is often challenging for younger students to grasp, because they are developmentally situated in an egocentric world and tend to have difficulty seeing beyond their own needs.

Where's the Value?

Expectations and challenge without value will result in only perfunctory success. Some students will do most anything you request of them simply because you request it—though the vast majority won't. In mathematics, once you go beyond basic arithmetic, most teachers are stumped if asked the relevance or value of a lesson. You know that you are on the lower end of the continuum for value if you consistently have difficulty answering *why* today's lesson is important. "Because it is a standard" or "Because it will help my students succeed with tomorrow's lesson" isn't good enough.

If you struggle with student apathy, you should reflect deeply on this aspect of your teaching. Students will often expend extraordinary effort if (1) they see value in the task and (2) they respect the teacher (see previous section). Ask yourself these questions:

- How do I convey the relevance of my lessons to students?
- How successful am I at getting students to buy into assignments?
- How can I better link relevance to my teaching even in lower-order areas like computational fluency, vocabulary proficiency, and general knowledge?

Where's the Power?

Is learning largely directed from you to the students, or do students play an active role in the process? If you tend to believe that students will succeed once you give them information, then your classroom is largely *teacher-controlled*. This is an antiquated instructional model; today, we know that students play a vital role in their own learning process beyond just taking notes, performing confirmatory activities that detail every step, or memorizing facts without learning why they're important.

Making Students Care

Before we can create a climate challenging enough for students to overcome apathy, we must make sure that we care about and deeply value what we are doing. Unfortunately, and likely not surprisingly, most Americans are unhappy with their jobs (Adams, 2014), and about half of all teachers leave the career altogether within five years (Neason, 2014). Research shows that feeling as though you are making meaningful progress is the single most important element in boosting emotions, motivation, and perceptions during the workweek (Amabile & Kramer, 2011). We must look every day for evidence that we are helping students learn. In seeking and then finding these often-small occurrences, we can begin to notice a pattern of positive progress.

The two primary intrinsic motivators for human beings are achievement and having our achievement recognized (McKeown, 2014). This recognition needs to be genuine. I have sat through enough ceremonies to know that trite prizes such as the "Busy Bee Reader" award, candy awards (Smarties for kids who are "smart" in all subjects, Baby Ruths for those who hit a home run with grades), or participation trophies don't do anything to promote challenge and excellence. Instead, how about looking students directly in the eyes and clearly telling them how and where they have pursued excellence and achieved great work? At first, this may mean simply picking out a well-worded phrase or a well-explained solution path. As excellence increases, you can engage in more complex conversations.

The Importance of Great Stories

What makes us care about a movie? According to Andrew Stanton (2012), a film director for Pixar, great stories affirm that our lives matter and provide us with a feeling of connection. Just as in good teaching, Stanton states that a good movie begins with the end in mind. As teachers, we need to be clear about how we intend to end our lesson, unit, or year. This requires working backward toward a starting point that draws students in by giving them a sense of anticipation.

Tom Burrell, the first prominent African American advertising executive in Chicago, can help us frame how to motivate students (Davis, 2002). As teachers, we rarely think about the sales or marketing aspects of our job, but if you think about it, we are "selling" what we teach every day. Burrell made the point that African Americans are more than just dark-skinned white people, and he worked to tailor ads for black audiences. He promoted a "positive realism" that highlighted more culturally and ethnically appropriate and relatable representations. He took common marketing images for Coca-Cola, Marlboro, and McDonald's and placed them in settings that were more relatable to African Americans—for example, moving from rural or suburban settings to urban settings. As educators, we too should be cognizant that learning and classroom interactions don't look the same to everyone.

Think about the things in life that have grabbed your attention, energy, or passion. Why did or do they grab hold of you? Then ask, why should your students care about your learning goals for them, and how will you encourage them to care? Remember that what holds value for one person may not do the same for someone else; you will need to explore ways to hook the curiosity of *all* students. Why does today's lesson *matter?*

The self-concept that helps determine our identity is greatly influenced by four psychological factors: *motivation* (what drives us); *perception* (our process of organizing and interpreting incoming data); *learning* (the actions we take to interact with the world); and *beliefs and attitudes* (the convictions we hold) (Rani, 2014). Giving students a reason to care about what they're learning influences student motivation and perception, which in turn result in more purposeful learning.

Making the World Better

In the late 1800s, society wanted a faster horse. Instead, on June 4, 1896, Henry Ford provided the public with a game-changing invention: the automobile. Although our accomplishments as teachers may not be as revolutionary, we should, like Ford, strive to make things better than they were before. Doing this helps provide us with purpose.

When we see that our guidance, support, or efforts are helping others in some way, we are encouraged to go further. Conversely, when we don't feel we can make a difference, we tend to sit quietly in the background. Only when we believe that our actions truly matter do we begin to speak up. We must advocate to ensure that all our students receive an equitable, high-quality educational experience. I am inspired by the four words Lucy Stone shared with her daughter 27 years before the passage of the 19th Amendment granting women the right to vote: "Make the world better." This is a great starting point to help focus our teaching every day. Real innovators strive to make the world better than it currently is, which often requires us to take risks—to stand up for a cause greater than ourselves. Whether the issue is bullying, academic integrity, or equality, we have to be prepared to speak up if we want to see a difference.

STOP TO REFLECT

- How will you step forward to make the world (and your classroom) better?
- How will the experiences, interactions, and lessons in your classroom reflect this change?
- Many students fear being seen or heard in front of their peers. How can you improve the environment so that students feel empowered to share, learn, and grow?
- How will all of your students become better both as scholars and as individuals as a result of your leadership?

Labels and Expectations

Assigning labels can help us categorize and make sense of the world around us. By labeling the colors of the rainbow, for example, we can better picture the continuous band of the visible spectrum and its millions of color gradations. Labels allow us all to share a common mental representation that we would not be able to share otherwise.

Educators use labels for students all the time: male, female, white, black, Asian, Hispanic, smart, slow, witty, struggling, overweight, attractive, charming, mean, poor, affluent, special needs, and so on. Although many of these may seem innocuous, the reality is that labels tend to elicit bias, whether conscious or unconscious, from those who use them.

An experiment by Robert Rosenthal and Lenore Jacobson (1992) provides a timeless example of the profound power of labels. During the spring term, researchers gave 1st and 2nd graders an IQ test and then randomly assigned them to two different groups. They told the teachers of students in one of the groups that those students were all "academic bloomers," but said nothing about the students in the other group. When the IQ test was given again at the end of the year, the students who had been labeled "academic bloomers" outscored those in the other group by an average of 10–15 IQ points. Researchers noted that teachers of students in the first group praised them more for their successes and ignored more of their errors than did teachers of students in the second group. These results should serve as a reminder that *all* students can and must be successful in our classrooms.

Experiments such as the one discussed above study what is known as *the expectancy effect:* the idea that perceptions and behaviors are influenced by our expectations or the expectations of others. Once a person believes something to be true, *that belief alone* makes it more likely to be true. I saw the expectancy effect in action first-hand when my daughter was guided into a "girl's" career track by her counselor. Although she had expressed interest in engineering as well as the health field, her counselor immediately and without further conversation narrowed her options down to nursing—a stereotypically "female" career path. Despite our best intentions, we all possess biases that can limit our effectiveness with our students.

We all would like to claim total impartiality when it comes to our interactions with students and others. However, our brains are often working in opposition to our heartfelt desires. A fear of differences is deeply ingrained in us as an innate protective mechanism, but we must acknowledge that we also have some control over it. Perhaps one way is to picture each of our students as our own child. There is nothing we value more dearly than our own children. Another approach would be to deliberately interact more with students who are different from us in some way until the difference recedes from our consciousness. As the expectancy effect shows, our expectations, whether low or high, are self-fulfilling. To improve the culture of challenge in your classroom, high expectations are essential.

STOP TO REFLECT

- What labels do you tend to assign to students?
- How do these labels hinder or benefit your students?
- How can you make sure that all your students thrive in your classroom?
- What do high expectations look like in your classroom?
- What does a "Goldilocks zone" of just-right expectations look like for each of your students?
- Do you consistently create a warm, welcoming climate through both words and actions? Evidence?
- How do you assess the quality of the work you assign? Do you assign too little or too much?
- Do you engage with *all* students? What does high expectations for *all* look like?

- What does praise look like for all students, and how do you differentiate feedback when responses are incorrect?

Questioning Questions

I contend that the questions we ask are far more important than the answers that we seek. Rich, thoughtful questions engage students, challenge claims, demonstrate depth of thinking, assess prior or current knowledge, and help students draw conclusions. Questions are like keys, unlocking the unknown and providing us with new realizations.

I recall being fascinated by the unknown as a child. In 5th grade, I was captivated by the fact that historians didn't know exactly how the Great Pyramids of Giza were built. I remember using various combinations of simple machines (wheels and axles, levers, pulleys) to model how nearly 70,000 stones could have been transported to the building site. Recently, I learned that newly discovered papyrus scrolls indicate the stones came by barge via canals that ran right next to the site. This simple idea was far from what I had envisioned as a child, since we only see a waterless desert surrounding the area today.

Good questions and powerful lessons engage us, arouse curiosity, inspire exploration, and challenge our thinking. They challenge students to look beyond easy solutions and tackle the tricky, the mysterious, the stubborn, and, sometimes, the uncomfortable. Highly effective teachers pose questions in a way that makes knowledge come to life, sparking delight and curiosity in students. The only truly bad questions are those meant to demean students by tripping them up. There is a difference between challenging student thinking and intentionally trying to mislead them. James E. Ryan (2017), one-time dean of Harvard's Graduate School of Education, suggests the following series of questions to ignite curiosity and challenge student thinking.

"Wait, what?" This is an effective way of asking for clarification, the first step toward truly understanding something. Before we adopt or advocate for a position, we must be clear on what it is. It is too easy to react on assumptions rather than facts. Use this question to frame perceptions accurately. In the classroom, ask, "Wait, what?" instead of affirming or correcting a student response—particularly if you want the student to elaborate on or rephrase his or her idea.

"I wonder why . . . ?" Questions that start this way help spark curiosity, which researchers have documented is conducive to health and happiness. When students are curious, they are likely to learn more and to retain more of what they study. (A variation, "I wonder if . . . ," also helps keep students engaged in the world.) "I wonder why . . . ?" is also good for sparking curiosity about ourselves. Why do we focus sometimes but get distracted at other times? Why do we like certain places, food, events, and people? Why are we excited and outgoing in some contexts and reserved and anxious in others? Why do we quickly lose patience with some people while demonstrating perpetual patience with others? "I wonder why . . ." is how children begin asking questions soon after they learn to talk. (The youngest children simply ask, "Why?")

"Couldn't we at least . . . ?" This question starter provides a good way to get unstuck and begin anew. For instance, I used it last semester to gauge my faculty's pressure points and found that what they wanted most were more opportunities to interact socially. By leaving the question open and incomplete (Couldn't we...?), we provide opportunities to spur innovation and creative thinking. When we use this formulation with students, we can learn about what motivates them. They may provide some outlandish responses, but at least you have something to work with that originates from the students themselves. "Couldn't we at least . . . ?" also helps us find common ground, asking all parties involved how to move forward together.

"What truly matters?" This is an essential self-reflective question that all teachers should ask themselves as they consider what is most important for students to know and be able to do. To answer the question, students need to synthesize facts, ideas, and knowledge to encapsulate the essence of the content they are being asked to learn.

STOP TO REFLECT

- What are three of the best questions you have recently asked your students?
- What makes your questions good, bad, or mediocre?
- What are the main goals of the questions you ask?
- What questions have you asked recently that helped you to attain these goals?
- Can you recall examples of questions you asked at the right time and ones you asked at the wrong time? How did you know the difference?
- What questions have you asked that created "aha" moments for your students?

What, Why, and Where Next

My daughter interrupted me the other day to ask what book I was reading. I described it to her, and she said it sounded boring. I asked her what topics excited her. She stared in confusion and answered, "I don't know, but your book still seems boring." The realization hit me: students are programmed to wait and be told what they will learn next as well as what they should enjoy. A potential question to explore with your students, then, is "What do you think is good, valuable, or important?" Push students to respond beyond vague descriptors. Is it something that makes us feel, think, or experience the world differently? If so, in what way?

Great salespeople ask three fundamental questions of their buyers:

1. "Is this product or service better than the one you currently have?" (creating a need)
2. "If you bought this today, would you use it?" (creating a sense of urgency)
3. "Debit, credit, or cash?" (closing the deal)

Perhaps the three fundamental questions we need to ask ourselves as teachers every day are as follows:

1. "What new idea, concept, problem, or creation do we need to investigate today?"
2. "Why is this important to know or be able to do?"
3. "What is the best way to engage students so that learning comes alive for them?"

Finally, three fundamental questions we should ask our *students* are these:

1. "What are you able to do that you were not able to do yesterday?" or "What do you know today that you did not know before?"
2. "Why does this really matter?" or "How is this learning connected to you or the real world?"
3. "Where do you need to go next in your learning?"

Asking *what, why,* and *where next* of students requires them to link their work to something of meaning and value. Aristotle provides the additional lens of persuasion to hook and engage your students. He believed that persuasion required trust (*ethos*), intellect (*logos*), and emotion (*pathos*). When we can appeal to all three elements, we are able to profoundly engage students. How did your last lesson (or how will an upcoming lesson) explicitly incorporate these three elements?

By the way, the book I was reading that my daughter said sounded boring—*Originals: How Non-Conformists Move the World* by Adam Grant (2017)—was one of the best books I had read in a while. Why? Because it was insightful and thought-provoking and provided new ways to tackle educational reform from a perspective outside education.

Perhaps a significant step would be for us to move away from trying to *educate* people to trying to *learn from* people. When we try to educate people, we thrust them into a passive role and shut down conversation. Learning from people opens up possibilities and requires participants to assume a more active role. When we learn from our students, we are more likely to understand their prior knowledge, current needs, personal perspectives, and cultural backgrounds. This is especially beneficial when addressing such politically charged issues as evolution, gun control, abortion, nuclear arms, and so on.

Consider climate change, for example. According to Leiserowitz and colleagues (2017), about 50 percent of Americans are now *very* or *highly certain* that global warming is occurring. Another data set suggests that 73 percent of Americans think there is significant evidence to support global warming, but that opinion is divided starkly between Republicans (50 percent) and Democrats (90 percent) (Borick, Rabe, Fitzpatrick, & Mills, 2018). I could *teach* students about the evidence for climatic change, test them on the facts, and move forward, suspecting that their opinions had not changed. It is not until we begin to discuss *why* students hold their opinions that we can truly begin to learn together.

This is not about indoctrinating students; quite the opposite, it is about ensuring that they form opinions based on the science. Students need to confront contradictions between opinion and fact. If I take the traditional approach to teaching and assume students have learned just because I have lectured or presented to them, I miss the opportunity to meaningfully and intentionally connect the learning experience to where they are as individuals—intellectually, emotionally, and developmentally. It is important that students, as citizens, base their opinions on accurate information and have opportunities to work through any misconceptions they may hold.

STOP TO REFLECT

- What have you done in the last week that was salesworthy?

- How have you engaged students and challenged their thinking?
- Where do you just provide information for students to memorize, and where do you expect them to engage more deeply?
- What are some creative ways to incorporate the *what, why,* and *where next* question frames in your classroom?
- Think of two or three instances when you felt the need to persuade your students or audience. Were you able to incorporate trust, intellect, and emotion in your argument? If not, what was missing?

Remember, people aren't born smart—they *learn to become* smart. Smart people read a lot, hang around other smart people who complement them, embrace mistakes, value all types of knowledge, and work very, very hard. How are you encouraging a culture that engages students in the above?

Nudging Success

We all want to succeed, so why don't we do it all the time? The answer is simple: we frequently behave irrationally, at the expense of our physical well-being, fiscal stability, and mental health. Rarely do we eat as well as we should or exercise as recommended. Richard Thaler, the 2017 winner of the Nobel Prize in Economics, has spent his life seeking to understand and change this irrational behavior. He is perhaps best known for his "nudge theory," which jump-started the field of behavioral economics. According to this theory, people often need subtle encouragement—a nudge—to achieve their desired goal. As an example, this theory has been successfully applied to help transform retirement programs from opt-in to opt-out defaults, resulting in millions more Americans setting up retirement accounts (Thaler & Sunstein, 2009). In another example, researchers (Wansink, Just, Hanks, & Smith, 2013) found that presenting students with apple slices rather than whole apples in the school cafeteria resulted in 73 percent more students selecting and eating more than half of the fruit.

The nudge theory has implications for the classroom, too. The fact that the brain continually seeks what is easiest presents an obstacle to challenging both our students and ourselves. We need to make it less comfortable for students to opt out of challenging work. For example, why not make honors classes the default in school, and opting out a step that students and parents must apply for? A nudge like this would set an immediate challenge for students to pursue learning at the highest level.

We can also use nudge theory to provide students with more choice and voice. In math, for example, instead of writing a single problem on the board for students to practice, why not write three problems at different levels of difficulty, encouraging students to pursue the most challenging problem first? Of course, this suggestion will work only if students see value in the lesson. If they perceive it as busywork, then they'll stick to the easy route—wouldn't you?

Teachers can use a nudge, too. We often stop students from learning right when it starts to go well. It's common for teachers to give their kids a "free day" when they're ahead of other classes. But if teaching is going so well, why on Earth would we slow down until the other classes catch up? The primary reason, as you know, is that it's easiest for us as teachers. One nudge to keep moving forward would be to use the opportunity for exploring a unique lesson format that you're thinking of adopting. Lock your smartphone away so you aren't distracted when you should be interacting with students. Perhaps move your desk chair so it's harder for you to stay behind your desk during class. Use the time you have to explore topics as deeply as you can.

Risks and Success

Getting your students to openly and honestly engage in learning—to take real risks—can be more of a challenge than asking them to jump out of a plane. Many students grow up in situations where self-protection is a means of survival; others are worried about losing social status in front of their peers if they make a mistake; still others have a success-at-all-costs mentality that keeps them from taking their chances, even if they have to sacrifice a portion of their grade in the process.

Before any students in your class will courageously step forward to take a risk, they need to feel that they are in a safe environment. Thus, the norms that you establish will be essential. We know that students learn more by participating than by observing, yet we frequently relegate them to the sidelines as we model how to solve a problem and expect them to do the same thing with only slight, if any, variations. There are times when this is necessary, but when learning through mimicry becomes the norm, we haven't allowed students to have control of their learning experiences.

Whether in school or in the workplace, psychological safety is the primary determinant of group or team success (Edmondson, 1999). Brené Brown, author of *Dare to Lead,* goes further: "Leaders," she writes, "must either invest a reasonable amount of time attending to fears and feelings, or squander an unreasonable amount of time trying to manage ineffective and unproductive behavior" (2018, p. 70). If our goal is to truly help develop the minds and hearts of our students, we must lead in a way that exposes our own vulnerability at times (Brown, 2015, 2018). English teachers often integrate vulnerability into their learning, such as by requiring students to write about personal experiences. It's important, in those cases, to acknowledge the risks that students have taken (e.g., by asking permission before sharing a student example). In classes outside the humanities, we can ask students to take risks by considering ethical questions such as gene therapy or trying a unique method to find a solution to a math problem, even if it doesn't work.

STOP TO REFLECT

- What are the norms in your classroom that encourage students to engage in learning while taking risks?
- Do your students know these norms? If so, have they bought into them? What is your evidence?
- How do you encourage those who are especially resistant to taking risks?
- How have you shared your own vulnerability with your students?

Building Critical Mass of Buy-In

To construct a solid building, we must begin with a sound foundation. Similarly, a strong classroom foundation that embraces challenge is built upon a critical mass of buy-in. And while teacher leadership is important for securing such buy-in, it is determined in large part by the leadership of students, which can and must be fostered.

Although you can't always determine who the student leaders will be in your class, you can have a dramatic effect on how they lead. Turning an otherwise negative leader into a positive role model can vastly change a classroom environment. Such role reversals are possible if you are intentional about your interactions. The students who carry the greatest respect and power in your class are not always the ones who come excited to recite Shakespeare, solve math problems, or develop their ability to speak a foreign language. To convert such students from adversaries of challenging instruction to allies, you must ensure that they feel sincerely appreciated and valued. A few side conversations between classes can plant the seeds of your respect for these students and their leadership. You might say something like, "Whenever you feel like giving up, maybe you can influence yourself and your peers to pause and ask *What if . . . ?* or *How could we . . . ?*"

Aligning Your Students' Perceptions with Yours

To be certain that your perception of your classroom culture is aligned with your students' perceptions, you must personally reflect on where you are and ask your students for their perspective. You can quickly draft an electronic survey for your students using software like Survey Monkey or Poll Everywhere to gather student data. Consider the following format and questions:

Please respond to the following statements using a scale from 1 to 5, where 1 = strongly agree, 2 = agree, 3 = neutral, 4 = disagree, and 5 = strongly disagree.

1. Expectations are high for all students in this class.
2. All students are challenged by the work in this class.
3. Teacher and students care greatly for one another.
4. Students encourage the success of one another.
5. Learning in this course consistently has purpose and value.
6. Learning in this course is relevant to student lives.
7. Students consistently have an active role in the learning in this class.
8. The teacher provides frequent opportunities for student input, inquiry, or innovation.
9. The teacher establishes clear norms that allow for safe risk taking.
10. Students feel that they can take risks during learning without being punished.

If you work with very young students or ones who have difficulty reading, you will likely need to rework the above statements a bit, read them aloud, or have students circle emojis representing the values of the 1–5 scale.

Once you've gathered students' responses, you can begin to see where perceived strengths and weaknesses exist. The final score should be the average of the scores for statements 1–2 (expectations), 3–4 (relationships), 5–6 (relevance), 7–8 (student autonomy), and 9–10 (risk taking). Set goals for growth in the areas where your score is strongest; for areas needing improvement, revisit the relevant sections of this chapter for guidance. Consider asking your students for their input on how to improve things. For example, if the score for the relationships questions is low, try brainstorming with students about how they might better encourage one another, and personally reflect on how you could better show that you care for your students.

STOP TO REFLECT

- Who are the key leaders in each of your classes? Remember, these are not necessarily the best or most positive students, but the ones with the power to influence others.
- How can you better utilize these students' abilities to further classroom goals?
- How can you begin to improve your relationship and interactions with those who have been using their leadership in negative ways?
- Is high-level challenge present in your classroom?
- What is the quality of the relationships that are fostered in class?
- To what degree is relevance integral to the curriculum?
- How much do your students exhibit autonomy?

Summing Up

This chapter pushed you to consider the culture that you have established in your classroom. What you glean from this reflection may affirm the excellence you have attained—or challenge you to better engage learners in the learning experiences you provide. In the following chapter, we move to the planning and assessment that will provide significant yet developmentally appropriate challenge.

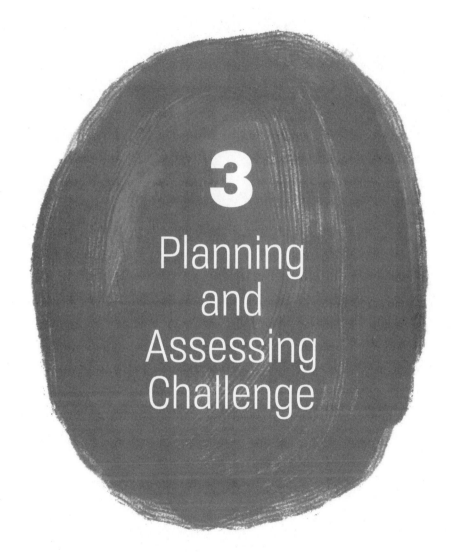

3

Planning
and
Assessing
Challenge

Michael Phelps, the record-breaking Olympian swimmer, used to devise mental "videos" of his upcoming races—from the feel of the water with his first stroke to the last kick of the leg at the finish—and watch them over and over in his head. Every night before sleeping and every morning upon awaking, he would revisit that mental video from beginning to end. This helped to motivate and guide him during workouts and kept him focused on the goal: victory.

The mental video that teachers rehearse in their heads doesn't need to be the same each day, but it's important to start an intentional habit of visualizing success. Once we envision in detail what success ought to look like, we can rewind the video as necessary for each step. To work, the video should include the habits, behaviors, experiences, culture, and interactions that spur success and achievement. If your goal is success with all types of students, then the video needs to include all types.

Routines help students develop automaticity of certain skills, allowing their brains to focus on new and challenging tasks. Given consistent daily practice, today's challenge becomes tomorrow's routine. Plan your video of success today, and watch it a few times at home tonight and again before your next class. Reengage students who have all but given up, and challenge those who are cruising, by intentionally planning for excellence.

In this chapter, we'll explore a variety of instructional approaches to help ensure that students are challenged as they learn.

STOP TO REFLECT

- You will only ever be as successful as your plan. What is your plan to achieve challenge and excellence in your next class?
- How close are you to achieving your vision of an ideal lesson? What gaps between actual and ideal need to be bridged, and how will you achieve that?
- What routines of challenge and excellence have you put in place?
- If you were to describe an ideal class from beginning to end, what would it look like? How would it begin and what would your role be? What questions would you ask to engage your students? What would your body language be like as you interacted with different kinds of students? What would your students be doing?

Standards

Do you carry your standards around like a ball and chain, or do they help guide the academic experiences in your class? In a comparative analysis of exemplary versus career teachers (Marshall, 2008), I found that exemplary teachers tend to see state and national standards as foundational to their teaching rather than obstacles to overcome, whereas the opposite was true for a majority of career teachers. At the same time, realize that standards are abstract for students and lack any real value for them.

Metacognition

Metacognition—thinking about our own thinking—is an excellent way for students to explicitly identify where they are struggling and where they are thriving. One way for teachers to engage students in metacognition is to enlist them in co-creating rubrics for major assignments. Keep things simple, perhaps by limiting the rubric to three categories (e.g., not yet, proficient, excellent) and keeping the list of assessed criteria short. After a few times, students will develop the skills to refine the rubrics they co-create, further strengthening their metacognition. If students are writing essays, another approach would be to ask them for help scoring two or three anonymous essays as a class. (Make sure to do this when the students are nearly, but not fully, done with their own essays, so they don't subconsciously pattern theirs on the ones they're scoring.) In addition to showing them a range of performance levels, such an exercise will likely provide students with ideas to help them improve their own work.

Technology

For the last 10 years or so, we have lived under the premise that more tech is better for learning. Unfortunately, this premise is rarely challenged, and rarely is it based on strong evidence. A large international study by the Organisation for Economic Co-operation and Development (OECD, 2015) found that heavy computer use actually leads to lower student outcomes in math, science, and reading. Used wisely, however, technology can enhance rather detract from learning.

In contrast to its findings on heavy computer use, the OECD found that *some* computer use was shown to be advantageous over no use at all. When computers are used as word processors, students tend to write more and better than they do by hand. Further, student outcomes significantly improved when computers were used to study or practice skills learned in class. This is largely because computers can provide immediate feedback and deliver differentiated responses much better than teachers can; for example, if students keep getting all the problems correct, many programs will automatically introduce more difficult problems to the mix.

Technology can and should be used to augment teaching, but it cannot be a substitute for human instruction. Too often, I see teachers provide a few introductory statements—sometimes on topic, many times not—before they direct students to their laptops or tablets to learn a lesson that was pre-published by an app. Although we may think this practice helps students to become more independent learners, the opportunity to challenge students to think deeply and interact with others is lost, and we are less able to tie each lesson to larger classroom goals.

Here's a better way to use technology with students. Provide them with a challenging question or real-world problem and have them work in teams to solve it. Only let students use the internet if the answer to the question can't easily be searched (e.g., "How many yards of concrete would be required for a building with three-inch concrete walls and six-inch concrete floors and X dimensions?"). Present a choice of problems at different levels of difficulty so that all students can feel engaged in the lesson.

Before implementing any technology-based experience in the classroom, think deeply about the value it does or doesn't provide to students. And when assigning homework, bear in mind that some students may not have access to the internet at home, and plan accordingly.

Differentiation That Promotes Challenge

Think of students as falling into one of the following three groups:

1. Struggling with the material
2. Achieving the expected outcome with a little scaffolding
3. Acing every assignment with little effort

Pre-assessment will help guide your decisions as you plan your lessons to help students in each group succeed. Then, work backward to plan your lessons, determining what proficient, advanced, and exemplary performance would look like before filling in the details of the learning experience. Although teachers typically award *A*s to students who merely demonstrate proficiency or compliance in their work, I believe high grades are only justified when expectations are exceeded.

Here are some examples, by subject, of lessons differentiated according to the three general challenge levels.

Science

The conservation principles (mass, matter, and charge) are fundamental in chemistry, and balancing chemical equations is one way for students to demonstrate their understanding of them.

For students in group 1 (proficient), ask a fundamental knowledge/skill question, perhaps with extra scaffolding.

> *Example:* Balance the following equation: $Na + Cl_2 \rightarrow NaCl$.
> (Helpful hint: In this equation, think of the arrow as being

like an equal sign—what you find on one side,
you must find on the other side as well. You may only
add coefficients—whole numbers in front of the standalone
element or molecule. Use the following as an example to
guide your decisions:
$H_2 + O_2 \rightarrow H_2O$ when balanced is $\underline{2}H_2 + O_2 \rightarrow \underline{2}H_2O$.)

For students in group 2 (advanced), increase the task complexity, providing support if necessary:

Example: Balance the following equation:

$P_4O_6 + H_2O \rightarrow H_3PO_3 + PH_3$

For students in group 3 (exemplary), make the task as challenging as possible while remaining developmentally appropriate:

Example: Balance the following equation:
$Cu + HNO_3 \rightarrow Cu(NO_3)_2 + NO + H_2O$

When teaching about density in science class, teachers will typically give students the formula for density and have them conduct a lab that confirms the formula. But students need to understand why density is important if they are to foster deeper conceptual understanding. One way to ensure this would be to have students compare items that have very different volume but the same mass (or vice versa).

Have students in group 1 determine the density of a block of metal. (*Note:* You may need to provide scaffolding to students. "What do we mean by density?" "How can we calculate density?" "What units are typically associated with its measurement?") In group 2, have students determine the density of a block of metal, blob of clay, or piece of plastic; for an extra challenge, ask them to complete the exercise for a type of plastic that has a lower density than water. They will have to be creative in using water displacement to measure the volume. In group 3, have students determine the density of a gas. Here the challenge is raised even further, as some students have yet to realize that gases have density and the solution will take more planning to figure out how to determine the mass (just placing a gas on a balance won't work).

English Language Arts

Find three paragraphs (or for younger students, three sentences), that are all well written but vary greatly in terms of complexity. Then, reverse-engineer each piece by adding errors in word usage, subject-verb agreement, or punctuation before giving them to students for correcting and refining. When reverse-engineering the original pieces, introduce errors common for your students' developmental level as well as a few unanticipated ones. Consider, for example, the opening line of *Peter Pan:* "All children, except one, grow up." An awkward reverse-engineering of this might read as follows: "Every body, including man, women, and children, do grow up at some point in their life's unless they are very unusual." You can also find good examples of writing in newspapers, blogs, books, or instruction manuals. It is exciting when a student or group refines a piece to be stronger or more powerfully worded than the original.

Mathematics

Although it is infrequently done in the same class, varying the complexity or challenge for different students is very manageable for math teachers. For instance, why should all students do problems 11–20 for homework if their development levels vary? A better option would be to have everybody try problems 1 and 11.

If students solve both problems with ease, then they should solve 21–27 (fewer but more challenging); if they solve 1 correctly but not 11, 7–17; and if they can't solve either 1 or 11, scaffold their practice until they can solve 1–10. To grade students, I would have them take a test made up mainly of questions in the 1–15 range of challenge, plus one or two from the highest level of challenge (questions 21–27) to distinguish *A*s from *B*s. (Another way to gauge students' levels of development is to write three levels of questions on the board for students to answer at the beginning of class.)

Too often, we become so preoccupied with ensuring that we're teaching to all learning styles that we forget to challenge students. We all need to learn to thrive in a variety of modalities, building on our strengths and improving our weaknesses. A variety of instructional approaches helps keep learning engaging for students while challenging different types of thinking.

What are three examples in your discipline of ways to engage students at different levels while keeping the core objective the same for all? Explore the critical ideas in your discipline and build up the levels of challenge in your lessons. When students feel that they can take risks without being penalized, they begin to raise their game.

Teaching for Higher-Order Learning

In science, teachers will sometimes ask students to design an experiment—after providing them with an intended purpose, procedural steps, data tables, and guiding questions. *Design* becomes *follow the steps*. A parallel exists in every discipline. But to develop the kind of higher-order learning that is typically assessed by state and national standards, teachers must engage students in actively exploring, gathering, and working through information in ways that require them to make difficult decisions. Two ways to facilitate this are using Webb's Depth of Knowledge levels and asking questions.

Webb's Depth of Knowledge

Webb's Depth of Knowledge (DoK) levels (Webb, Horton, & O'Neal, 2002) link depth of understanding to the scope of a learning activity. The four DoK levels are as follows:

1. Recall and Reproduction
2. Basic Skills and Concepts
3. Strategic Thinking and Reasoning
4. Extended Thinking

In level 3, students are expected to generalize patterns, analyze data and form conclusions, develop logical arguments, synthesize information from a single text, verify results and claims, consider multiple perspectives, and design investigations. By level 4, students should be able to illustrate how historical themes are interrelated, analyze complex or abstract themes, model real-world situations, and synthesize information from multiple sources. Following are some examples of instructional activities in different disciplines, adjusted for the different DoK levels.

Level 1

- Correct the punctuation, if necessary, for the following five sentences.
- Restate Newton's three laws of motion.
- Identify which of the following are complementary angles.

- Highlight the boundaries of the Roman Empire on the map.

Level 2

- Give an example of a time when Atticus Finch from *To Kill a Mockingbird* displayed courage.
- Explain how to go from *A* to *B*. [This general example can be used in math (e.g., procedures), cartography (e.g., directions), science (e.g., laboratory procedures), English (e.g., formation of a strong essay), or social studies (e.g., the process of a bill becoming law).]
- Interpret the meaning of the slope on the graph showing rate versus time.
- Which of the following individuals or groups were Confederate sympathizers?

Level 3

- Write a persuasive essay on an issue related to climate change that is supported with details and examples.
- Predict a logical near-term course of the stock market or specific commodity based on current trends.
- Develop a mathematical model for calculating the area of complex figures that incorporate multiple shapes.
- Identify common historical misconceptions and propose a solution for minimizing them.

Level 4

- Analyze the texts read over a semester to determine underlying themes across genres.
- Synthesize what you've learned to solve a real-world problem using a provided data set but no obvious algorithm.

- Design and conduct an investigation focusing on one of the global challenges.
- Write a historical narrative that details the Vietnam era using multiple sources from multiple perspectives.

Asking Questions

By far the most common types of questions from students are those asking for some sort of confirmation (e.g., "Is this correct?" "What are we supposed to do?"). If your students ask these types of questions more than others, they are probably just playing the game of school. Students can learn quickly that they don't have to listen to instructions or read directions if they can just pepper the teacher with questions. To prevent this habit from forming, tell students they may work in groups for the first five minutes of an assignment but are not allowed to ask you questions. Another option is to "sell" your responses to questions for points, with higher points going to the highest-level questions. Your goal is to stifle students' low-level questions and encourage deeper reflection on their work. Have examples of high-level questions around the room or on lab counters to model deeper questioning for students. When students begin asking rich, thought-provoking questions, didactic interchanges become rich, conversational learning experiences.

Here are some higher-order question starters that can be used across disciplines:

- What happens when we change the parameters of . . . ?
- Will this behavior persist when X occurs?
- Does this only occur when we . . . ?
- Would the same conclusion result if . . . ?
- Is there a more powerful way to express . . . ?

- How does this tie into what we've already learned or what you learned in X class?
- Can we create a rule or model for X that can be applied to most cases?

Notice that these examples quickly take us into the real world. This is often the piece we struggle with, yet it is essential for engaging our students.

Make an audio recording of your next lesson. How well did your questioning align with lesson objectives or the goal of challenging students at high levels? Did the lesson begin with a challenge or an essential question that was not quickly solvable? Did the lesson both scaffold and challenge student learning? If so, where? What thinking were students responsible for, and what were they just parroting back? Prior to your next three lessons, script out a few key questions to use and consider ways you might encourage students to ask higher-level questions.

Balancing the Neat but Impractical with the Messy but Realistic

The real world is a messy, incomplete system where questions and uncertainties far outnumber answers. By contrast, classrooms are largely devoted to gathering facts, absolutes, and unquestionable truths. Since the days of John Dewey, educators have argued that schools need to better represent reality. Some teachers think that students need to know all kinds of facts and algorithms before they can hope to address complex real-world problems. But even from a very young age, we are exploring these complex problems. So why not let students in early childhood classrooms investigate such issues as homelessness, poverty, human rights, and the environment? If we want students to learn to think at higher levels and become engaged citizens and critical consumers, we must ensure regular opportunities for them to practice, grow, and discover in the messy gray areas where few absolutes exist.

If students have for years been playing the game of school, following a set of rules and expectations devoid of real-world application, changing their habits will take time. A balance between consistency and variety is key. I recently heard a group of 6th grade students ask their teacher at the beginning of class whether she was going to "talk at" them today or if they were going to "get to figure things out" instead. The latter is the type of learning that we want for our students, and has been shown to raise achievement in both content knowledge and process skills across races and genders (Marshall, 2013; Marshall et al., 2017).

Researchers have identified three strategies—*retrieval practice, spaced practice,* and *interleaved practice*—that promote long-lasting knowledge retention and are generalizable across disciplines (National Academies of Sciences & Medicine, 2018).

Retrieval practice can dramatically improve knowledge retention (Karpicke, Blunt, & Smith, 2016; Lipko-Speed, Dunlosky, & Rawson, 2014). When we are just reviewing information, we are inclined to think we understand something simply because we're familiar with it, whereas retrieval practice forces our brains to make connections that extend beyond mere familiarity, which promotes active learning. By contrast, just watching lectures or reading through notes is a passive mode of learning in which the brain disengages as soon as things are familiar. Further, when we practice retrieval, we inevitably fail to retrieve all the information we seek, alerting us to what we don't yet fully understand. The goal of retrieval is to ensure that the fundamentals are in place when working on the bigger picture. Examples would include asking students to recall historical dates or to describe, explain, or summarize key concepts.

A type of retrieval practice, **spaced practice**—the practice of studying over time rather than all at once—is hugely beneficial for long-term learning (Carpenter, Cepeda, Rohrer, Kang, & Pashler, 2012; Kang, 2016). Unfortunately, cramming and mass practice are the norm in schools. In math class, we tend to give problem after problem using the same formula, as if the real world were so kind as to always provide the exact algorithm we need. There is a point to this kind of mass practice, but it shouldn't be the primary pattern of learning in any classroom. In spaced practice, the greatest amount of studying occurs around the initial learning of an idea and tapers off until the test comes, by which point students are very well prepared.

Interleaved practice has been shown to have significant benefits in many learning situations (Carvalho & Goldstone, 2014; Rohrer, 2012). Whereas a teacher using mass practice might have students practice addition problems over and over again, for example, one using interleaved practice would have students working with both subtraction and addition (or even subtraction, addition, multiplication, and division). Although the students in the first scenario may develop their addition skills sooner, the ones in the second scenario are more likely to know whether addition or subtraction is necessary for a given problem. In many disciplines, related terms are more easily understood when learned together rather than in isolation.

The value of interleaving becomes fully clear when it comes time for a summative assessment. If you haven't used interleaved practice during the year, only the students who are already good at synthesizing information will do well, and those who struggle even a bit will feel as though they are taking a quantum leap into the unknown.

STOP TO REFLECT

- What are three to five major real-world connections to your discipline?
- Pick one real-world connection to incorporate in your teaching. How will you work to scaffold learning for students?
- What are some tangible ways for you to engage students in the messiness of the real world while meeting standards?
- How are you ensuring that knowledge retention is maximized in your class? Where is spaced or interleaved practice appropriate for your class, and how can you improve its use in your classroom?
- What types of practice do you regularly use, and what types should you be adding to your repertoire?

Learning That Is Appropriately Challenging and Engaging

A science teacher once asked me for help understanding why some of her students had not done well on her test. After examining the test, I noticed that she started many of her test questions with a blank. This practice presents great difficulty for struggling readers, who often don't know how to start their writing. If my primary goal is to engage students in writing, then removing that obstacle allows students to immediately begin improving their writing fluency. If some students in your class are more creative than others, one idea is to have the former provide starting points for the latter—by writing the beginning of a story during a creative writing lesson, for example. Or students might work on an adventure story with multiple paths, with all students, individually or in groups, contributing to the best of their abilities. Peer editing helps everybody grow. (This approach works with nonfiction as well.)

In a math or science class, you could have advanced students write their own test questions on key concepts. Now that they have demonstrated knowledge, can they apply it independently? Give them parameters—for example, questions must provide a range of challenge and not merely be fact-based. When possible, they should address a real-world scenario. The goal is not getting to where you are today but getting to where you will be tomorrow and the day after that. Growth!

Three ways to ensure your teaching is sufficiently challenging and engaging are to have students consider multiple perspectives, summarize and draw to express their understanding, and develop explanations for their answers.

Considering Multiple Perspectives

Students who learn how to see and understand things from multiple perspectives become more innovative, creative, flexible, diplomatic, and empathetic. In a society filled with self-selecting social media feeds that perpetuate confirmation bias at every turn, we as teachers must help students learn to challenge assumptions and listen to underrepresented and differing viewpoints. Here are some ways to practice this strategy in different disciplines.

- *Math:* Pursue multiple solution paths for individual problems.
- *Science:* Show how collecting multiple samples increases confidence in a hypothesis.
- *History:* Consider the perspectives of different population groups on historical events.
- *English language arts:* Write from the perspective of different literary characters.
- *Physical education:* Analyze different possible plays or formations.

Summarizing and Drawing

Studies show that summarizing is linked to effective learning (National Academies of Sciences & Medicine, 2018). Summarizing requires students to distill their personal understanding of a topic. It can be simple and quick to implement, such as having students summarize the last five minutes of discussion with a neighbor. Drawing is similar, with students creating a visual representation of their understanding. When it is used to summarize or synthesize ideas, drawing is a powerful tool, particularly for those who struggle for the words to express their thoughts (e.g., young children or English language learners). Drawings and more elaborate representations like 3-D models are especially useful for visualizing abstract ideas or concepts that aren't visible to the naked eye (e.g., showing how molecules behave differently in solids versus liquids).

Developing Explanations

To challenge students beyond defining, restating, and summarizing, prod them to explain and justify their answers. In math, for example, students might write a narrative explanation of solving a problem, forcing them to think carefully about each step in the solution path and ingraining the practice in their mind. Good frames for explanations include the following:

- Why do you think . . . ?
- What was your reasoning behind . . . ?
- Tell me more about . . . .
- How did you arrive at this conclusion?

STOP TO REFLECT

- In the next week, what topic in your class do you think would be most advantageous for students to study from multiple perspectives?
- How would studying something from multiple perspectives strengthen students' depth of knowledge?
- How can you use summarizing and developing explanations in an upcoming lesson?

Purposeful Measurements

"Water, water, everywhere, / Nor any drop to drink." The famous line from Samuel Coleridge's *The Rime of the Ancient Mariner* makes me think of all the data in our schools today. The line could be rewritten for today's educators as "Data, data, everywhere, / Wonder what to think." We have become so fixated on measuring everything that we forget to pause and ask what the data really tell us. Perhaps the key is to shift from *telling* to saying, "Tell me more." When we tell, students only know they are supposed to remember what we said. When we have students tell instead, we are challenging their thinking.

I set expectations in the *B+/A–* range for successfully completing an assignment. To move beyond this, students must provide additional value. For example, on a writing assignment, I may expect students to use proper syntax, include five citations, and present at least three convincing points to support claims. A student meeting all these benchmarks would receive 90 percent (less deductions for omissions or errors). To achieve the remaining 10 percent, students need to go the extra mile: provide more than five citations or three supporting points, perhaps.

Many students, particularly those accustomed to achieving the highest possible grade on assignments, balk at this system at first, but it raises the bar for everyone. If you choose to implement something similar, have students explicitly state for you what, if any, value-added work they have done on their assignment. For instance, in math, students might add a column next to a solution where they provide a narrative explanation of how they solved one or more of the problems.

Encourage students to come up with their own ways of adding value to assignments. Some examples might include proposing additional experiments for solving a problem, providing study tips to classmates, suggesting links between the material and current events, or connecting material across disciplines.

STOP TO REFLECT

- Think about your most recent assessment. Was it based on what was easiest to implement and grade, or did it authentically measure student learning? What evidence do you have to support your claim?

> • The goal of assessment is to provide effective and
> timely feedback to students regarding their growth,
> but there are often ways to achieve efficiency as
> well. How can you improve the efficiency of your key
> assessments while maintaining their effectiveness?

Going Beyond Knowledge: Thinking, Character, Habits, and Perspectives

When we think of challenging our students, the common default is to believe that challenge is solely and inextricably linked to knowledge and skills. But we can also challenge students in ways that improve their thinking, character development, positive habit formation, and perspectives. Let's take a moment to explore how and where you currently challenge your students in these areas. This information can provide a baseline from which you can establish goals or next steps to raise your game in a given area.

Thinking. Thinking and cognition is a broad category, so let's consider more targeted areas related to how we lead and improve thinking among our students. There are multiple mechanisms that we use to challenge thinking, including the following:

- *Metacognition:* Do you ask students to think about their own thinking (e.g., "Where do you struggle the most? Excel with the topic?")?
- *Questioning:* What questions do you ask that require students to engage in higher-order thinking?
- *Application:* Do you provide students with opportunities to apply what they learn to real-world situations? Do you encourage students to think creatively?

- *Assessment:* Do you frequently and thoughtfully implement formative assessment to challenge thinking? If so, does this assessment help you chart student growth or inform your next instructional steps?

Character. Powerful thinking is clearly desirable, but it is not solely sufficient for attaining challenge and excellence. In his 1837 speech titled "The American Scholar," Ralph Waldo Emerson stated, "Character is higher than intellect. . . . A great soul will be strong to live, as well as strong to think." In fact, character helps define one's personality. Respect and responsibility are two examples of ideals we strive for in supporting our students' character development. How do you challenge the development of student character in your classroom?

Habits. To paraphrase Zig Ziglar, character is what gets us out of bed, commitment is what moves us to action, and discipline is what enables follow-through. Follow-through is essentially the habit that reinforces individuals as they strive for excellence. Habits become our behavior, which in turn frames our character. We seek to cultivate strong positive habits, such as perseverance, preparedness, metacognition, taking responsibility for one's actions, curiosity, and engagement. Such habits become part of daily learning and support the thinking that encourages challenge and excellence in all students. Many of our high-performing students have already established positive habits that foster learning and personal growth. How are you encouraging the success of the other students through positive habit formation?

Perspectives. To learn or understand anything deeply typically requires us to consider multiple perspectives. This is difficult for very young students, but it should become an expectation for students as they grow and develop past the early grades. As we have discussed, the confirmation bias our society has fallen prey to makes such an enterprise challenging but all the more important. When we seek to understand others before we try to be understood ourselves, we begin to employ the idea of perspective. Understanding the perspective of others helps us construct stronger collaborations, thereby creating synergies where the group is far stronger than the individual. How do you promote the practice of considering multiple perspectives in your classroom or discipline?

STOP TO REFLECT

- In what ways have you challenged the thinking of your students in the past week or unit of study? Where could you improve?
- Do you differentiate your level of challenge to suit different students' developmental needs? If so, is this differentiation something you do infrequently or regularly?
- How do students respond to challenges—do they shut down, struggle, engage, push each other? How do you wish students to respond? What steps can you take to achieve this end?
- Can you identify any missed opportunities for introducing greater challenge in your teaching?
- Where have you provided opportunities for students to wrestle with character development in class?
- In what ways does your discipline help students build strong character?

- Can you identify some specific missed opportunities for character development over the past term?
- Where in your lessons is student character being challenged or tested?
- How have you encouraged strong habit formation among students, particularly those who need it most?
- Do you model strong habit formation and address the topic explicitly with your students? Be sure to be consistent: if you encourage a habit of timeliness, for example, you must be timely yourself.
- Can you pinpoint essential habits that some or all your students are missing? What can you do to help students form these habits?
- How are your students being challenged to think about issues, ideas, or solutions from multiple perspectives?

These questions are designed to show that challenge goes beyond memorization of facts or speed of computation, and to encourage more intentional thinking about how, when, and where you are challenging your students in these important areas. You can use these questions to review past units of study and, more important, to help you proactively incorporate these facets in upcoming units.

Summing Up

In this chapter, we looked at instructional approaches to ensure that students are challenged as they learn. Developing a plan and accompanying formative assessment for guiding challenging and rigorous learning sets the stage for increased success with our students. In the following chapter, we'll explore how to proceed in executing this vision.

4

Facilitating and Implementing Challenge

We all want to be successful with our students, but how we define that success varies greatly. Too often, we get trapped into advocating for one end of a dichotomy: traditional versus progressive, creativity-focused versus knowledge-focused, discovery learning versus direct instruction. In this chapter, we'll look at ways to enact challenging lessons and work through common obstacles. I believe that to successfully challenge all learners today, we need to seek a balance among three core aspects of learning: knowledge acquisition, curiosity development, and critical thinking advancement.

Knowledge Acquisition

A small sample of the knowledge acquired in schools would include primary colors, multiplication tables, key historical events, the basic parts of speech, the names of chemical compounds, Spanish vocabulary words, the Pythagorean theorem, the parts of a persuasive essay, and the formula for velocity. Teaching strategies that help to build knowledge include lecture, drill and practice, and direct instruction.

Central to school though it is, helping students to acquire knowledge is only a fraction of what teachers must do to ensure success. After all, computers can dispense knowledge even more efficiently and effectively than we can. But while computers are full of information, they have yet to become curious; Google will tell us the answer to almost any question we ask, but it cannot tell us the questions that need to be asked.

Curiosity Development

Both the questions that we ask as teachers and the questions that arise from students are vital to deep learning. Teacher questions provide the tenor of the room, indicating whether learning will be solely knowledge-based or if it will further engage learners by sparking their curiosity. Student questions can serve as a measure of the culture of learning. A preponderance of clarifying questions ("What are we supposed to do next?"), questions seeking affirmation ("Is this right?"), and fact-probing questions ("What is the answer to number 5?") indicate learning that only skims the surface, whereas metacognitive questions ("I understand how to get here in the solution, but where do I go next in the solution path?"), curiosity-centered questions ("Why is it that when ... ?"), and critical thinking questions ("How would the analysis change if we varied ... ?") tell us that students have taken charge of their learning and are using knowledge to spur deeper engagement with the material.

So which comes first, knowledge or curiosity? Neither; they must occur simultaneously. When we are curious about the world around us, knowledge makes sense and has value. At the same time, curiosity cannot really exist in the full absence of knowledge. Einstein would not have been interested in time travel or general relativity if he knew nothing about physics.

Historically, humankind has been very curious. Between the ages of 2 and 5, children tend to ask about 40,000 exploratory questions, many of them seeking to understand why things are as they are (Harris, 2012). Yet we appear to be in the second major suppression of curiosity in recorded time. The first, known as the medieval period, progressed for centuries in Europe as the Church and others sought to stifle curiosity. Today's problem is rooted in an abundance of knowledge, thanks to technology and an assumption that teachers are always correct and ready with an answer. We have fallen into the trap of letting quick answers trump the pursuit of the unknown in numerous arenas. In school, by about 3rd grade, students begin to trade their innate curiosity for compliance with drill and rote learning. In politics, polar extremes rail against each other instead of seeking to understand and compromise. Social media shows us what we like and are familiar with instead of inspiring us to learn about other ideas, cultures, or perspectives. And many teachers feel that their own creativity is stifled by their school's obsession with standardized test performance. To make matters worse, this suppression of curiosity doesn't yield positive results. Although a focus solely on surface-level knowledge acquisition may increase test scores in the short term, long-term success in student learning is seen when students are actively engaged in learning via guided inquiry practice that promotes creativity and critical thinking (Marshall & Alston, 2014).

Critical Thinking Advancement

When we engage in critical thinking, the meaning and value of knowledge become clear as we apply and analyze what we've learned. Unfortunately, much of what passes for critical thinking instruction is really just knowledge-based work (e.g., asking students to evaluate something "independently" while providing all the steps for them). Of course, students must develop at least some knowledge base before they can become proficient at higher-order thinking. Once students have begun developing their knowledge base, however, it is appropriate to jump back and forth between knowledge-based and critical thinking instruction.

STOP TO REFLECT

- Which aspect of education do you tend to focus on most: knowledge acquisition, curiosity development, or critical thinking advancement?
- What do you see as the benefits and disadvantages of relying too heavily on that aspect?
- Do you see a need to better balance the three aspects in your practice? If so, what are concrete steps you can take to achieve that balance? If not, what evidence do you have that suggests your approach challenges all students? What might prevent you from making the necessary changes, and how can you minimize these obstacles?

Challenge and Failure

Failure. Just saying the word stirs up negative emotions. Perhaps it is the fault of our education system that an aversion to failure has been bred in us. From an early age, students are taught that there is one right answer, and that the teacher has it. But this approach inhibits creative, innovative learning. The question for teachers is how to fit such learning into the context of a standards-based world.

Are *challenge* and *failure* antonyms, or are they synonyms? I contend that not all failure is equal. Certainly, *failure to start* is a major roadblock to challenge. Unfortunately, it is also very common in many of our schools, with many students feeling that they haven't failed if they haven't tried. Failure to even attempt a challenge is more of a defense mechanism than anything.

Then there is the failure we encounter when things don't go as expected while we are learning. Unlike failure to start, *failure in pursuit of knowledge or solutions* is largely synonymous with challenge. We experience this kind of failure when we are vigorously engaged in curiosity: an error message when programming software, an invention that doesn't hold up, a story rejected by the literary magazine, or just finding ourselves at a dead end after a lengthy search.

We tend to punish failure rather than reward it. Google X executives tried a different approach by giving standing ovations and bonuses to teams for their "moonshot" attempts, even when the company ended up shutting down a program; wisdom, they believed, resides in knowing when to continue and when to stop (Huckman, Lakhani, & Myers, 2018). As an academic, I have learned that failure is part of the job. I have received lots of red ink from editors, sometimes asking for major revisions, sometimes pointing out minor issues, sometimes flat-out rejecting a manuscript. Although humbling, research and writing can be very rewarding: every resubmission is an improvement on the original, and my high expectations for myself continue to pay off. (To be completely honest, a part of me questions whether I can succeed with each new book project I undertake, yet each final product seems to be stronger and more insightful than the last—at least, I hope it is!) Too many of us are paralyzed when it comes to making improvements because we fear that our performance might worsen in the process. This can also be true for students who have been winning at the game of school—they know what to do to earn good grades but aren't willing to push beyond that for continued growth.

If we don't want our students to fear failure, then we need to stop fearing it, too. When I work with groups of instructional coaches, teachers, and leaders, I find that few, if any, of them consider them-selves to be risk takers. If you are not willing to challenge yourself in some substantial way, then it's unrealistic to expect your students to. Take a simple example: if you want to score the most points in basketball, then the easiest thing to do is to stand right by the hoop and shoot layup after layup. In the short term, you will achieve your goal, but in the long term, you will not know how to succeed from elsewhere on the court. The same holds true in class. We can teach addition and practice adding single digits over and over again, but unless students know how to apply and analyze these skills, they are missing out on deeper thinking and problem solving. Here are some examples of ways to incorporate failure into the learning experience as a positive in different disciplines.

English language arts. Have students share their writing before and after editing to show how the product transformed, through failure, for the better. This strategy also helps develop students' metacognition.

History. "Failures" in history are subjective and are often reas-sessed as new perspectives or developments come to light.

Science. Understanding sources of error and how to reduce them as well as retesting to see if values can be improved are ways to investigate failure in the laboratory.

Let's be honest. Even the best hitters in baseball only hit about one in three times at bat; top basketball players score about 50 percent from the court on a good night; authors are turned down far more often than they are published; more businesses fail than succeed. Isn't it time we stopped bubble-wrapping our kids in an effort to protect them from failure, if it's something they'll encounter throughout their lives? To do otherwise is borderline unethical, preparing students to crumble when things don't go well.

Of course, we want students to succeed on the final test or project—the classroom equivalent of game day. But we also want students to learn from rather than fear mistakes. How you process and share your own mistakes determines the type of culture you will promote in your classroom. Like most people, I have experienced many setbacks in life, from poor athletic performances to relationship breakups. In the end, however, every failure made me a better person. We all get stuck at some point—if we don't, we've probably never been truly challenged. The question is what to do when we get stuck. For those who excel in school, problems that are not easily answerable can produce fear and anxiety. It might be helpful to tell these students that not trying for fear of getting stuck is the only thing you will consider "truly failing."

Rarely is something "one and done" in the real world. If you fail your driver's test, you can take it again. If your dinner turns out less than ideal, there is always tomorrow night. If the job interview goes awry, there will be other jobs to apply for. I believe the same should be true of summative assessment. Rather than just say to students, "You get what you get," teachers should provide them with the opportunity to improve their scores by correcting their errors, showing knowledge in a different way, or retaking the test or resubmitting the project.

STOP TO REFLECT

- How do you guide students who can't get "unstuck" or fail to even start?

- Where do students have the opportunity for second chances in your class?
- Are there times when second chances are not appropriate?
- How do you help your students work through failure and the accompanying emotions?
- Do you and your students take opportunities to reflect on failed attempts as you both strive toward success?

Prioritizing

Lao Tzu wrote, "To attain knowledge, add things every day. To attain wisdom, subtract things every day." Our lives are full of hurry; we rush from one thing to the next, getting overly stressed in the process. Part of this stress can be avoided by prioritizing and identifying the purpose and value of what we do. The word *priority* entered the English language around 1400. It remained a singular noun until the 1900s, when the plural form of the word began to be used. Today, most of us have multiple priorities that all demand our attention.

How often do we hold our students responsible for distilling their work, focusing on a single core idea? In an age of ubiquitous and instantly available information, it is vital for students to learn how to synthesize data. Ask them to clearly state in one sentence the focus of a given lesson or to articulate how what they've learned will apply to their future learning. Have them restate core ideas to a classmate. Require a one-sentence summation of the day's lesson as an exit slip for leaving class.

Clarity of purpose is essential for promoting excellence. Without clarity, we experience confusion, stress, frustration, and, ultimately, failure. Once we understand the real purpose of what we're learning, we can begin to see its value and meaning—and we can start prioritizing. Our highest priority should be the thing that holds everything else together, the reason we are here doing what we do. If you're teaching U.S. history, for example, you should go beyond the course title "U.S. History from 1865 to Present." Your highest priority might be a theme or a guiding question, such as "How does our learning from past events inform our decisions in the present and future?" The class could periodically revisit this overarching question to glean relevance and context for why a given topic is important for them to know about today. Second on the hierarchy of importance should be the five to eight things that are most critical for students to know and be able to do by the end of your class. Standards and objectives should come third in importance.

STOP TO REFLECT

- What would the learning hierarchy look like for you as a professional? Think about your job and determine what is of primary importance (what frames your identity as a teacher), of secondary importance (skills that you need to do very well), and of tertiary importance (things that should be done well but are not necessary to success).
- What are three specific ways that you can engage students in concisely stating what the key priority of a lesson is?
- What is the most valuable contribution that you provide for your students? Once you know the answer to this last question, you will know the areas that you need to address further.

Inquiry: Right-Side-Up Teaching

Inquiry-based learning, active learning, problem-based learning, project-based learning—all these approaches rely on the constructivist principle that learning increases when students actively engage with the learning process. When we challenge students to grapple with an idea before showing the solution path, they are forced to build from their prior learning while assimilating new thoughts, ideas, concepts, or perspectives. When students wrestle with a problem or question before the answer is explained to them, they develop a *need to know* (see p. 21). Even medical schools, such as the ones at the University of Vermont and Case Western Reserve University, have moved from a lecture focus to more active models of learning.

Here are some examples of ways to engage students in thinking and discussion rather than just replicating the solution we give them.

Math. Begin with an error and see if students can work in groups to figure out where the error occurred. For example, you might place the following sequence on the board:

If $x = y$, then 2 = 1

1: If $x = y$
2: $x^2 = xy$ [multiple both sides by x]
3: $x^2 + x^2 = x^2 + xy$ [add x^2 to both sides]
4: $2x^2 = x^2 + xy$ [combine like terms]
5: $2x^2 - 2xy = x^2 + xy - 2xy$ [add $-2xy$ to both sides]
6: $2x^2 - 2xy = x^2 - xy$ [combine like terms]
7: $2(x^2 - xy) = 1(x^2 - xy)$ [factor both sides]
8: $2(x^2 - xy)/(x^2 - xy) = $
   $1(x^2 - xy)/(x^2 - xy)$ [divide both sides by $(x^2 - xy)$]
9: $2 = 1$ [simplify]

Did you find the error? It may not be so obvious. It occurs in line 8: If $x = y$, then $(x^2 - xy)$ would equal 0. If that is true, then you cannot perform the division function stated, because it is impossible to divide by 0.

Social studies. A good challenge for social studies would be to have students investigate, gathering as much evidence as they can, whether and to what degree Russia influenced the 2016 U.S. presidential election. In our era of social media, how do we begin to unravel what is and what isn't trustworthy and what our own biases are? For example, if you get your news from Facebook or Google, you are prone to confirmation bias, because algorithms continually tailor these sites to our views. If you lean left politically, it is more likely than not that opinions in your newsfeed do as well. This does not make the newsfeed true or false, but it does make it biased. Unfortunately, we're not very good at identifying bias; one study found that fewer than 10 percent of students were able to determine the bias of a source (McGrew, Ortega, Breakstone, & Wineburg, 2017). We can help our students become better consumers of information by modeling lateral reading, comparing search engine results, or analyzing Wikipedia entries.

History. Have students engage in historical inquiry, providing them with primary sources appropriate for the different developmental levels in your class. Pose a question, establish a historical context, and provide guiding questions as needed, or work with the class to develop questions. Historical inquiry promotes engagement and critical thinking as students investigate historical questions, evaluate evidence, and construct claims supported by evidence. Starting with a primary document for students to read is a great way to begin inquiry in a history class. Instead of just telling students what is important and then supporting it with a few quotes from a primary document, start the other way around. Begin with an excerpt from the U.S. Constitution, a court ruling, or a peace agreement, and have students grapple with its implications, interpretation, or relevance.

STOP TO REFLECT

- What are some ways to engage students before you formally explain a lesson?
- How can you encourage thinking, engagement, discourse, and persistence?
- What questions help you to guide these experiences?
- What is the role of student presentation and discussion in this process?
- How should you or can you connect engagement to the formal understanding of content?

One of These Things

A puzzle or mystery creates a disequilibrium that our mind seeks to resolve, helping to ensure a memorable learning experience. One mystery made famous by *Sesame Street* is the "One of These Things" exercise, where the goal is to figure out which item is not like the others and why. Here are two examples of ways to use "One of These Things" in class.

English language arts. Which of the following quotes does not belong, and why?

1. You've got to climb to the top of Mount Everest to reach the Valley of the Dolls. (Jacqueline Susann, *Valley of the Dolls*)

2. It was the best of times, it was the worst of times, it
   was the age of wisdom, it was the age of foolishness,
   it was the epoch of belief, it was the epoch of incre-
   dulity . . . (Charles Dickens, *A Tale of Two Cities*)
3. Friends, Romans, countrymen, lend me your ears;
   I come to bury Caesar, not to praise him.
   (William Shakespeare, *Julius Caesar*)
4. In my younger and more vulnerable years my
   father gave me some advice that I've been turning
   over in my mind ever since. (F. Scott Fitzgerald,
   The Great Gatsby)

All but number 3 are the first lines to famous works, but the truth
is that there could be several correct answers to this question. The
point is to engage students in thinking and exploring. As the lesson
proceeds, the focus might turn to writing an essay, in which case
these examples could model powerful first sentences.

Math. Which of the following does not belong, and why?

1. A circle roughly the size of a half-dollar with a dime-
   sized circle inside. Both circles share the same center.
2. A circle roughly the size of a half-dollar with a
   dime-sized square inside. Both shapes share the
   same center. The region between the square and
   the circle is shaded.
3. A triangle roughly the area of a half-dollar with a
   dime-sized square inside.
4. A circle roughly the size of a half-dollar with a
   dime-sized square inside. Between the square and
   circle is another circle roughly the size of a quarter. All three shapes share the same center.

5. A circle roughly the size of a half-dollar with a dime-sized square inside. Both shapes share the same center.

There are several possible answers to this question, but one solution is best. Keep pushing until you figure it out.

The World Is Not Clear-Cut

In math, answers often seem static and straightforward. With the following activity, you can upend this common conception. Start class by saying, "Sometimes the world is not as clear-cut as we believe. I am going to place a problem on the board, and I will give you a moment to figure it out on your own. Then, everyone will respond in unison with their answer. Ready? 9 plus 8 equals. . . ." Students will confidently respond with "17." But what if you wrote "9 + 8 = 5" on the board as they answered? They would be confused, of course. Now let's say you followed the same steps with the following problems and answers:

$$9 + 8 = 5$$
$$2 + 3 = 5$$
$$7 + 7 = 2$$
$$6 + 6 = 12$$
$$7 + 8 = 3$$

The pattern here corresponds to modulus arithmetic, sometimes called "clock math," in which the response reflects the time arrived at when adding to a number on an a.m./p.m. clock. You might place students in groups to see if they can determine the pattern and, if so, whether they can apply their knowledge by creating two problems (with solutions) that follow the pattern. You may need to provide scaffolding to assist students. If they are stuck, you could provide a hint by asking, "If I work for eight hours today, starting at 9:00 in the morning, what time do I finish working?"

You're not trying to "trick" students with this activity; rather, the goal is for them to explore possibilities, consider multiple perspectives, and challenge their thinking. Computational fluency and conceptual understanding are important, but you can get an answer to almost any problem by putting it into software such as Mathematica or Excel. This exercise is about getting students in the habit of thinking beyond algorithms so that they will persevere when faced with real-world challenges.

Debunking Myths

What do Eratosthenes, Columbus, and a lunar eclipse have in common? All three have contributed to our acceptance of the Earth as spherical rather than flat. Perhaps you could ask students to research Eratosthenes, Columbus, or lunar eclipses and share the insights that they provided as to the true shape of our world. For example, Eratosthenes employed science and mathematics to calculate the circumference of the Earth.

STOP TO REFLECT

- What are some ways for you to increase intrigue and mystery in your lessons?
- How could you introduce content to your students using inquiry-based lessons for greater engagement?
- Students will have a tendency to shut down if they don't know how to proceed or understand teacher's expectations. How will you help them begin to change

their approach to grappling with unknowns in your classroom?

Return to the math example in the "One of These Things" section on pages 99–100. If you didn't solve it, go back and do so now. If you were not intrigued enough to stop and solve it the first time, why was that? Think about how you would have needed to change the problem so that it would have been engaging for you. If you've skipped over examples because they don't reflect your area of expertise, you are missing a great opportunity to learn beyond your walls, and you miss the opportunity to explore how to tailor material so that it suits you and your students.

Now, for the actual solution to the problem. Figure 1 does not belong because it is the only figure without a square. Figure 2 does not belong because it is the only figure with a shaded region. Figure 3 does not belong because it is the only one with no circle. Figure 4 does not belong because it is the only figure with three shapes. Figure 5 is the only one that belongs in all cases. Students will often select one of the first four figures and neglect the fifth. We often need to challenge students to go beyond the obvious or intuitive.

Challenging Parents

How do we challenge parents in thoughtful and encouraging ways—and how do we work with challenging parents? Let's begin with the first question. Teachers must work with parents to help them be encouraging but also know when to step away so their children can establish good habits, rebound from failure, and build persistence.

To help establish habits, parents of younger children can read with them 20 minutes each evening, gradually working toward them reading independently. If the parents themselves can't read very well, perhaps a sibling could help, or parents could learn to read alongside their children. Although this latter approach requires parents to share a weakness, it sends perhaps the most powerful message of all: "Learning is so important that I am willing to go on that journey with you."

Parents might also help their children review their most challenging subjects for a few minutes each evening. Even if no homework is assigned, they might provide their kids with rich cultural experiences such as trips to the museum, a state or national park, an aquarium, or the state capitol building. Parents should model achieving success after hard work, help their kids celebrate growth, and offer encouragement where the learning curve is steep; what they should *not* do is solve challenges for them. Students must see more than just the end products of success; they need to experience the journey of achieving it.

STOP TO REFLECT

- How do you engage the parents of your students in creating a challenging learning environment to complement what occurs in class?
- What supports do you provide to parents (e.g., conversation starters, sample questions to help them review)?
- How are you proactive in your communication with parents so that they become allies rather than adversaries?

Skin in the Game

Some teachers run toward professional learning opportunities, while others avoid them like the plague. Why the difference? Habit? Personality? Growth versus fixed mindsets? No skin in the game is one reason for running away from professional development. The number of no-shows for professional development is always higher when everything is paid for and no commitment is required from teachers (e.g., sharing their learning with the team or creating a product of some kind).

Do your students have skin in the game? After all, education is free to them, and they know it will help them. Perhaps the game is one that our brains play on us. From an evolutionary standpoint, brains are wired to free up the "hard drive" (long-term memory) when possible, achieving a default resting state. This is perhaps to ensure that our brains are ready to respond on a moment's notice, which made sense for our ancestors, whose survival in dangerous conditions depended on it. Today, however, our default resting state involves scanning Facebook or Instagram. Why not use this time instead to write a journal entry reflecting on our day's practice and consider improvements for tomorrow?

I will tell on myself for a minute. Recently, I fell into the trap of checking my phone for messages at every opportunity and always having my e-mail open on my desktop. But because this game of constantly being plugged in results in a distracted existence, I vowed to change things. First, I changed my phone habit: I turned off all notifications and vowed not to check e-mail on my phone for a week while on vacation. Now, I look only a few times a day, allowing me to be more present where I am. On my computer, I now have e-mail closed except for the three or four times a day I spend focused only on that. This intentionality has freed up cognitive space and energy while also allowing me to work through my e-mail queue more quickly and more thoughtfully.

STOP TO REFLECT

- Do you and your students have skin in the game? If so, what are some of the obstacles preventing success?
- What are some changes that you would like to make with your students?
- Do you have a colleague who is willing to tackle changing a habit with you (it doesn't have to be the same habit)? This would allow you to hold each other accountable.
- How will you reward yourself as you achieve your target?
- Simply put, how are you invested in improving your performance, and what are the steps that will make this happen?

Summing Up

As teachers, we seek to inspire, motivate, and grow our students. To maximize success, students must be challenged beyond the normal status quo or passive gathering of knowledge. When done well, the lessons we facilitate can create rich opportunities for students to thrive. How has your instruction challenged all students in appropriate ways today?

Conclusion

This book has focused on providing reflection questions, examples, and support for improving the challenge and excellence in your classroom with all your students. My hope is to spur a conversation around fostering greater challenge for students. We each bring unique experiences and abilities to our work, so the path to growth will be different for everyone. In what area do you need to do the most work to thrive: culture, planning, assessment, or implementation? Focus on one area and dig deep.

To truly improve, you must commit to moving beyond your current experiences. Celebrate what is going well, but also target those things that can and must change for challenge, rigor, and excellence to be present in your classroom. When you dive deep to explore the questions in this book, you will keep coming back with evidence of where you are succeeding and where you need to do better.

Remember that the only true failure is a failure to act. What actions will you engage in today and tomorrow to take the next steps? As you finish each week and prepare for the next, ask yourself these questions:

- What worked well this week, and why?
- Where was challenge present, and where can it be introduced?
- What must happen next week so that all my students succeed?

You need to ensure that you are committed to having students grow and thrive in your class. I encourage you to develop a set of promises to make to your students at the beginning of each year (revisiting them when you get in a rut). Nothing is more discouraging to students than a teacher's broken promise, so make sure you are deeply committed to keeping every one. It can be extraordinarily empowering for students to know how committed you are to helping them succeed.

So what promises should we make to our students? Here are a few suggestions:

- I will never give up on you.
- I won't allow you to give up on yourself.
- I trust you and respect you.
- I will ensure that you can succeed and excel in this class.

References

Adams, S. (2014). Most Americans are unhappy at work. *Forbes*. Retrieved from https://www.forbes.com/sites/susanadams/2014/06/20/most-americans-are-unhappy-at-work/

Amabile, T. M., & Kramer, S. J. (2011). The power of small wins. *Harvard Business Review*. Retrieved from http://hbr.org/2011/05/the-power-of-small-wins/

Anderson, L. W., Krathwohl, D. R., Airasian, P. W., Cruikshank, K., Pintrich, P. R., & Wittrock, M. (Eds.). (2001). *A taxonomy for learning, teaching, and assessing: A revision of Bloom's taxonomy of educational objectives*. New York: Addison Wesley Longman.

Bligh, D. A. (1998). *What's the use of lectures?* Bristol, UK: Intellect Books.

Bloom, B. S. (1956). *Taxonomy of educational objectives: Cognitive domain*. New York: David McKay.

Borick, C., Rabe, B., Fitzpatrick, N., & Mills, S. (2018). As Americans experienced the warmest May on record their acceptance of global warming reaches a new high. *Issues in Energy and Environmental Policy*. Retrieved from http://closup.umich.edu/files/ieep-nsee-2018-spring-climate-belief.pdf

Bradbury, N. A. (2016). Attention span during lectures: 8 seconds, 10 minutes, or more? *Advances in Physiology Education, 40,* 509–513.

Brown, B. (2015). *Daring greatly: How the courage to be vulnerable transforms the way we live, love, parent, and lead*. New York: Penguin.

Brown, B. (2018). *Dare to lead: Brave work. Tough conversations. Whole hearts*. New York: Penguin.

Brown, P. C., Roediger III, H. L., & McDaniel, M. A. (2014). *Make it stick: The science of successful learning*. Cambridge, MA: Belknap Press of Harvard University Press.

Bunce, D. M., Flens, E. A., & Neiles, K. Y. (2010). How long can students pay attention in class? A study of student attention decline using clickers. *Journal of Chemical Education, 87*(12), 1438–1443.

Carpenter, S. K., Cepeda, N. J., Rohrer, D., Kang, S. H., & Pashler, H. (2012). Using spacing to enhance diverse forms of learning: Review of recent research and implications for instruction. *Educational Psychology Review, 24*(3), 369–378.

Carvalho, P. F., & Goldstone, R. L. (2014). Putting category learning in order: Category structure and temporal arrangement affect the benefit of interleaved over blocked study. *Memory & Cognition, 42*(3), 481–495.

Cian, H., Marshall, J. C., & Qian, M. (2018). Inquiry classroom patterns of student cognitive engagement: An analysis using growth curve modeling. *Journal of Science Teacher Education, 29*(4), 326–346.

Davis, J. F. (2002). Enterprise development under an economic detour? Black-owned advertising agencies, 1940–2000. *Journal of Macromarketing, 22*(1), 75–85.

Eagan, K. (2016). *The American freshman: Fifty-year trends, 1966–2015.* Los Angeles: Higher Education Research Institute, Graduate School of Education & Information Studies, University of California.

Edmondson, A. (1999). Psychological safety and learning behavior in work teams. *Administrative Science Quarterly, 44*(2), 350–383.

Emerson, R. W. (1837). *The American scholar* [Speech]. Retrieved from http://irsc.libguides.com/ld.php?content_id=45731779

Grant, A. (2017). *Originals: How non-conformists move the world.* New York: Penguin.

Harris, P. L. (2012). *Trusting what you're told: How children learn from others.* Cambridge, MA: Harvard University Press.

Hattie, J. (2009). *Visible learning: A synthesis of over 800 meta-analyses relating to achievement.* London: Routledge.

Hess, K. K., Carlock, D., Jones, B., & Walkup, J. W. (2009). *Cognitive rigor: Blending the strengths of Bloom's taxonomy and Webb's depth of knowledge to enhance classroom-level processes.* Dover, NH: National Center for Assessment.

Huckman, R. S., Lakhani, K. R., & Myers, K. R. (2018, March). X: The Foghorn decision. Harvard Business School Case 618-060. Retrieved from https://www.hbs.edu/faculty/Pages/item.aspx?num=54400

Kang, S. H. (2016). Spaced repetition promotes efficient and effective learning: Policy implications for instruction. *Policy Insights from the Behavioral and Brain Sciences, 3*(1), 12–19.

Karpicke, J. D., Blunt, J. R., & Smith, M. A. (2016). Retrieval-based learning: Positive effects of retrieval practice in elementary school children. *Frontiers in Psychology, 7,* 350.

Leiserowitz, A., Maibach, E., Roser-Renouf, C., Rosenthal, S., Cutler, M., & Kotcher, J. (2017). *Climate change in the American mind: March 2018.* New Haven, CT: Yale Program on Climate Change Communication.

Lipko-Speed, A., Dunlosky, J., & Rawson, K. A. (2014). Does testing with feedback help grade-school children learn key concepts in science? *Journal of Applied Research in Memory and Cognition, 3*(3), 171–176.

Luthar, S. S., & Latendresse, S. J. (2005). Children of the affluent: Challenges to well-being. *Current Directions in Psychological Science, 14*(1), 49–53.

Marshall, J. C. (2008). An explanatory framework detailing the process and product of high-quality secondary science practice. *Science Educator, 17*(1), 49–63.

Marshall, J. C. (2013). *Succeeding with inquiry in science and math classrooms.* Alexandria, VA: ASCD & NSTA.

Marshall, J. C. (2016). *The highly effective teacher: 7 classroom-tested practices that foster student success.* Alexandria, VA: ASCD.

Marshall, J. C., & Alston, D. M. (2014). Effective, sustained inquiry-based instruction promotes higher science proficiency among all groups: A five-year analysis. *Journal of Science Teacher Education, 25*(7), 807–821.

Marshall, J. C., Smart, J. B., & Alston, D. M. (2016). Development and validation of Teacher Intentionality of Practice Scale (TIPS): A measure to evaluate and scaffold professional development. *Teaching and Teacher Education, 59,* 159–168.

Marshall, J. C., Smart, J. B., & Alston, D. M. (2017). Inquiry-based instruction: A possible solution to improving student learning of both science concepts and scientific practices. *International Journal for Science and Mathematics, 15*(5), 777–796.

McGrew, S., Ortega, T., Breakstone, J., & Wineburg, S. (2017, Fall). The challenge that's bigger than fake news: Civic reasoning in a social media environment. *American Educator, 41*(3). Retrieved from https://www.aft.org/ae/fall2017/mcgrew_ortega_breakstone_wineburg

McKeown, G. (2014). *Essentialism: The disciplined pursuit of less.* New York: Random House.

McSpadden, K. (2015, May 14). You now have a shorter attention span than a goldfish. *Time.* Retrieved from http://time.com/3858309/attention-spans-goldfish/

Merikangas, K. R., He, J. P., Burstein, M., Swanson, S. A., Avenevoli, S., Cui, L., et al. (2010). Lifetime prevalence of mental disorders in U.S. adolescents: Results from the National Comorbidity Survey Replication—Adolescent Supplement (NCS-A). *Journal of the American Academy of Child & Adolescent Psychiatry, 49*(10), 980–989.

Middendorf, J., & Kalish, A. (1996, Fall). The "change-up" in lectures. *TRC Newsletter, 8*(1). Retrieved from https://citl.indiana.edu/files/pdf/middendorf_kalish_1996.pdf

National Academies of Sciences & Medicine. (2018). *How people learn II: Learners, contexts, and cultures.* Washington, DC: National Academies Press.

Neason, A. (2014). Half of teachers leave the job after five years. Here's what to do about it. *Huffington Post.* Retrieved from https://www.huffingtonpost.com/2014/07/23/teacher-turnover-rate_n_5614972.html

Organisation for Economic Co-operation and Development (OECD). (2015). *Students, computers, and learning: Making the connection.* Paris: OECD Publishing.

Rani, P. (2014). Factors influencing consumer behaviour. *International Journal of Current Research and Academic Review, 2*(9), 52–61.

Rohrer, D. (2012). Interleaving helps students distinguish among similar concepts. *Educational Psychology Review, 24*(3), 355–367.

Rosenthal, R., & Jacobson, L. (1992). *Pygmalion in the classroom: Teacher expectation and pupils' intellectual development.* New York: Irvington.

Ryan, J. E. (2017). *Wait, what? And life's other essential questions.* New York: HarperCollins.

Stanton, A. (2012, February). *The clues to a great story* [TED Talk]. Retrieved from https://www.ted.com/talks/andrew_stanton_the_clues_to_a_great_story

Talbott, S. M. (2007). *The cortisol connection: Why stress makes you fat and ruins your health—And what you can do about it.* Alameda, CA: Hunter House.

Thaler, R. H., & Sunstein, C. R. (2009). *Nudge: Improving decisions about health, wealth, and happiness.* New York: Penguin Books.

Wansink, B., Just, D., Hanks, A., & Smith, L. (2013, May). Pre-sliced fruit in school cafeterias: Children's selection and intake. *American Journal of Preventive Medicine, 44*(5), 477–480.

Webb, N. L., Horton, M., & O'Neal, S. (2002). *An analysis of the alignment between language arts standards and assessments in four states.* Paper presented at the annual meeting of the American Educational Research Association, New Orleans, LA.

Index

About the Author

Jeff C. Marshall, PhD, is a professor and associate dean for research and graduate studies in the College of Education at Clemson University. He has received the Presidential Award for Excellence in Mathematics and Science Teaching, published 5 books and more than 60 articles, and given more than 130 presentations in the last 12 years alone. He also serves as a consultant for school districts, universities, and grant projects throughout the United States.

Marshall received his BS from the University of Central Oklahoma and an MS and PhD in Curriculum and Instruction from Indiana University. He can be contacted at Clemson University, 105 Tillman Hall, Clemson, SC 29634. Phone: 864-656-2059. E-mail: marsha9@clemson.edu.

Related Resources

At the time of publication, the following resources were available (ASCD stock numbers appear in parentheses).

Print Products

The Highly Effective Teacher: 7 Classroom-Tested Practices That Foster Student Success by Jeff C. Marshall (#117001)

How to Plan Rigorous Instruction (Mastering the Principles of Great Teaching Series) by Robyn R. Jackson (#110077)

Increasing Rigor in the Classroom (Quick Reference Guide) by Barbara Blackburn (#QRG119044)

Now That's a Good Question! How to Promote Cognitive Rigor Through Classroom Questioning by Erik M. Francis (#116004)

Qualities of Effective Teachers, 3rd Edition by James H. Stronge (#118042)

Reading, Writing, and Rigor: Helping Students Achieve Greater Depth of Knowledge in Literacy by Nancy Boyles (#118026)

For up-to-date information about ASCD resources, go to www.ascd.org. You can search the complete archives of *Educational Leadership* at www.ascd.org/el.

DVD

What Rigor Looks Like in the Classroom (ASCD DVD) by Robyn Jackson (#616018)

ASCD myTeachSource®

Download resources from a professional learning platform with hundreds of research-based best practices and tools for your classroom at http://myteachsource .ascd.org/.

For more information, send an e-mail to member@ascd.org; call 1-800-933-2723 or 703-578-9600; send a fax to 703-575-5400; or write to Information Services, ASCD, 1703 N. Beauregard St., Alexandria, VA 22311-1714 USA.

The ASCD Whole Child approach is an effort to transition from a focus on narrowly defined academic achievement to one that promotes the long-term development and success of all children. Through this approach, ASCD supports educators, families, community members, and policymakers as they move from a vision about educating the whole child to sustainable, collaborative actions.

Rise to the Challenge relates to the **engaged**, **supported**, and **challenged** tenets.

For more about the ASCD Whole Child approach,
visit **www.ascd.org/wholechild.**

WHOLE CHILD
TENETS

1 **HEALTHY**
Each student enters school healthy and learns about and practices a healthy lifestyle.

2 **SAFE**
Each student learns in an environment that is physically and emotionally safe for students and adults.

3 **ENGAGED**
Each student is actively engaged in learning and is connected to the school and broader community.

4 **SUPPORTED**
Each student has access to personalized learning and is supported by qualified, caring adults.

5 **CHALLENGED**
Each student is challenged academically and prepared for success in college or further study and for employment and participation in a global environment.